John
Calvin

WOMEN OF FAITH SERIES

Amy Carmichael   *Isobel Kuhn*
Corrie ten Boom   *Joni*
Florence Nightingale   *Mary Slessor*
Gladys Aylward   *Susanna Wesley*

MEN OF FAITH SERIES

Andrew Murray   *John Calvin*
Borden of Yale   *John Hyde*
Brother Andrew   *John Newton*
C. S. Lewis   *John Paton*
Charles Colson   *John Wesley*
Charles Finney   *Jonathan Goforth*
Charles Spurgeon   *Luis Palau*
D. L. Moody   *Martin Luther*
E. M. Bounds   *Oswald Chambers*
Eric Liddell   *Samuel Morris*
George Muller   *William Booth*
Hudson Taylor   *William Carey*
Jim Elliot

WOMEN AND MEN OF FAITH

John and Betty Stam
Francis and Edith Schaeffer

OTHER BIOGRAPHIES FROM BETHANY HOUSE

Autobiography of Charles Finney
George MacDonald: Scotland's Beloved Storyteller
Hannah Whitall Smith
Help Me Remember, Help Me Forget (Robert Sadler)
Janette Oke: A Heart for the Prairie
Miracle in the Mirror (Nita Edwards)
Of Whom the World Was Not Worthy (Jakob Kovac family)

John
Calvin

Dr. William Lindner

BETHANY HOUSE PUBLISHERS
MINNEAPOLIS, MINNESOTA 55438

John Calvin
Copyright © 1998
William Lindner, Jr.

Cover art is adaptation of an image, courtesy of the
H.H. Meeter Center

Cover by Dan Thornberg,
Bethany House Publishers staff artist.

Published by Bethany House Publishers
A Ministry of Bethany Fellowship International
11300 Hampshire Avenue South
Minneapolis, Minnesota 55438
www.bethanyhouse.com

Printed in the United States of America by
Bethany Press International
Minneapolis, Minnesota 55438

ISBN 0-7642-2005-5

For

Nicole, Rachel, and William, III

*"I shall be your God
and your children's God . . ."*
(GENESIS 17:7).

DR. WILLIAM LINDNER, JR. holds a D.Min. in renewal, with an emphasis on the ministry of Andrew Murray. A pastor in the Evangelical Presbyterian Church, he lives in Mt. Pleasant, Michigan, with his wife and three children.

Contents

1

Origins of a Revolutionary

Quickly! Quickly! Another second and the door will give way! They've almost made it through!" The muffled cries of the wanted man's companions could be heard in the street below.

Everything inside the small student apartment was in panic-stricken disarray. Two people were busy tying rags and sheets together for a makeshift rope. Another was quickly collecting incriminating papers—those too dangerous to risk being found were tossed into a growing blaze in the fireplace. Somewhat disoriented, the student being sought was dragged to the window by the others. A Parisian graduate, he was disguised as a vinedresser, though his pale skin, thin build, and awkward gait hardly contributed to the disguise. It was dark though, and time was short, the hasty escape more urgent than well-planned.

"Quickly!" came the cry once more. They literally pushed their friend out the window as he clung to the sheets for dear life. His desire for escape was nearly squelched by the sheer terror of dangling over the ledge above the street. That desire was rekindled when he heard the door come crashing in under the weight of the king's soldiers. They began ransacking the apartment in a desperate attempt to find their culprit, while the Parisian's friends fought back with little effect.

Sliding to within five or six feet of the ground, the subject of the king's animosity jumped free and scrambled off into the night. He was a wanted man, a refugee if he escaped, and all because of his connection to a speech filled with revolutionary ideas. It had hardly been what he wanted or could have imagined, but God must have had a purpose in it all. He must trust God for tomorrow and make good his escape now.

Who was this inflammatory radical? This student revolutionary fleeing Paris only a step ahead of the police? He was none other than John Calvin, remembered today as one of the founders of the Protestant Reformation, a pastor in Geneva, Switzerland, and author of Bible commentaries and a book called *The Institutes of the Christian Religion*.

There are many good historical reasons to doubt nearly every detail of the legend regarding Calvin's midnight escape from Paris after the All Saints' address by his friend Nicolaus Cop. Quite accurate, though, are the persecution, revolutionary ideas, sudden flight, and danger at the heart of the tale. Indeed, they give us a truer picture of John Calvin than many of the modern images that present him as a cold, stern, legalistic academic who was the dictator of Geneva and responsible for the burning of an innocent man. Try to look past all the legends and meet the sixteenth-century man who presented ideas that changed the course of Western civilization.

———

Noyon is a tiny village located in the fertile, wheat-producing plains of the Picardy region of France. It has a modern-day population of just over 13,000 people. Noyon is located eighty-five miles north/northeast of Paris, fifteen miles beyond the city of Compiegne, where Joan of Arc was captured in battle and where the World War I Armistice was signed. Situated on the small river Verse, the town's heritage began in the fourth century as a Roman way station. In French history, it is remembered as the place where Charlemagne was crowned in 768 as joint King of the Franks.

The real identity of the town was related to its ecclesiastical character. In 531 it became the seat of a line of Catholic bishops that would continue for almost thirteen-hundred years until the French Revolution. One seventh-century bishop—Eloi—would become a saint, the patron of blacksmiths. Between 1150 and 1290, a cathedral was constructed in his honor. Somber and austere, the building looks back in architectural style, more the Romanesque of preceding ages than the Gothic style that was beginning to emerge at the time. This same backward perspective seemed to hang onto the tiny village well into the sixteenth century.

When Gerard Calvin moved there from an outlying village in 1481, it was with the hope of a more prosperous life for himself and his family. He apparently achieved this purpose by leaving behind the manual trades of his ancestors and becoming a secretary to the bishop in Noyon. Hard work, ambition, and skill enlarged his circle of influence over time. He became a fiscal agent for the county and an attorney for the governing board that oversaw the affairs of the cathedral. Soon he was accepted as a member of the *bourgeoisie*, the local aristocrats—wealthy, influential people that formed the effective governing class of the area.

Sketchy records show that Gerard and his wife Jeanne Lefranc had five sons. Two died very early. The oldest, Charles, would follow in his father's footsteps, or perhaps shadow, and become very involved in the business of the bishop at Noyon. The youngest son, Antoine, would one day move to Geneva, Switzerland, where he would enter the book business and become involved in the city government, much as his father did in Noyon. But the middle son, Jean, is the one that draws our interest. Better known as John Calvin, he would undergo a Protestant awakening and become a pastor in Geneva. From that position, he influenced the course of history.

John Calvin was born in Noyon on July 10, 1509. Outside the sleepy village, several currents of change were gathering to form a storm not yet seen. The flourishing of art, philosophy, and culture that we now call the Renaissance had been underway for over a century. Johan Gutenberg had developed the printing press in 1450. Christopher Columbus had discovered a new world less than two decades before Calvin's birth, and in less than one decade afterward, a German monk named Martin Luther would nail his Ninety-Five Theses to the door of Wittenberg Cathedral with the hope of debating abuses in the Catholic Church. Indeed, Europe was ripening for change, but inside this rural French village, one could hardly tell. The Renaissance seemed to have passed by this tiny town. The place of John Calvin's birth was traditional and determined in every appearance.

Little is known about the family life of the Calvins when John was a child. His father was clearly working hard to climb the ladder of influence and respectability. He was a force to be reckoned with, considered by most to be hard and somewhat severe in character.

Gerard's wife, Jeanne Lefranc, was the daughter of a wealthy innkeeper who had retired to Noyon and been accepted into the *bourgeoisie* and city council. Reports speak of her exceptional beauty and deep, traditional Catholic piety. Sadly, she died while John was still young, no older than six.

Gerard soon remarried, though even less is known about his second wife. She became the mother of two daughters, half sisters to John. One, Marie, would follow her half brother to Geneva. Of the other there is little, if any, historical record.

During this time, John began his studies with the best the town had to offer. His ambitious father had him schooled with the sons of one of the most prominent families in the area, the Montmors. This probably meant that even in Noyon, John would move in with the family and share life with the children and their tutor. Later, Calvin would mention this time and family in a dedicatory letter to his first book, a 1532 scholarly commentary on Seneca's *De Clementia*: "I owe you all that I am and have. . . . As a boy I was brought up in your home and was initiated in my studies with you. Hence I owe to your noble family my first training in life and letter."

John did well, picking up his lessons quickly. It was said that he had "a fine intelligence, a natural readiness to comprehend the humanities," and that he surpassed his schoolmates, "thanks to his quick intelligence and excellent memory." These early years of genteel schooling also gave John Calvin an aristocratic refinement that would later distinguish him from the more roughhewn reformers like Luther and Zwingli.

> The upbringing of Calvin and the Montmors was no doubt conventional in the late medieval manner. They would know whippings in plenty. They would be treated as undersized adults from whom was demanded early responsibility. They would face the peril of not only the dangerous childhood illnesses but also the plagues that frequently ravaged Noyon. They would become resigned to the physical discomforts of an age that had not learned to look after itself. But with all this, there was the security of a stable society as one year followed another in predictable course. The home of these children who began their lives with the sixteenth century was watched over by the cathedral on their right hand and Sainte-Godebert on their left, two stone symbols of the permanence of the

church of God, two living centers of the all-pervasive activity of the church of God in his world.[1]

For all the ambition of his father and John's quickness, life in Noyon was provincial and unassuming. His father, Gerard, moved up in life by excelling within the structures of the past, not by inventing new ones. He trained his three sons in the conventions of the known world, not the dreams of a new.

---

[1]T. H. L. Parker, *John Calvin: A Biography* (London: J. M. Dent and Sons, Ltd., 1975), 2.

2

An Education for the Future

Gerard Calvin was a man who intended to advance his family's fortunes. He found ample opportunity for this advancement within the administrative structure of the most pervasive institution of his day: the Roman Catholic Church. We would be remiss to think of Gerard's career as religiously motivated or involving pastoral work, as it is called in modern times. There was no preaching or administrating of the sacraments as part of his position. He was a layperson who worked for the church authorities. He applied his obvious skills to the business of the Roman Catholic Church, functioning in the vast bureaucracy and serving the myriad of institutional needs that remained in the wake of medieval society where the Church was involved in every aspect of life.

It was only natural that when the time came to direct the future of his sons, Gerard looked to the Church, the same source of his own opportunities for advancement. Charles, the eldest son, was made a chaplain of the Noyon cathedral in 1518. His brother John was only nine. Keep in mind that this appointment had no religious function similar to our modern understanding. It was a position with an income handed out to a deserving or well-connected person, apart from their ability. By way of example, church historian Philip Schaff records the rise to power along this same route by Pope Leo X, the pontiff who initiated Martin Luther's excommunication.

> Pope Leo X received the tonsure as a boy of seven, was made archbishop at eight, and cardinal-deacon in his thirteenth year (with the reservation that he should not put on the insignia of his dignity or discharge the duties of his office until he was sixteen), besides being canon in three cathedrals, rector in six parishes, prior in three convents, abbot in thirteen additional abbeys, and bishop of Amalfi, deriving revenues from them all![1]

This sort of patronage was very common throughout Europe at this time, so Charles' appointment was nothing out of the ordinary. It was, rather, a sign of Gerard's growing influence.

In like manner, Gerard secured a portion of the revenue from the cathedral chaplaincy, in 1521, for his second son, John, while he was still only twelve. By this time, Cortez had landed in Mexico and Martin Luther was in the throes of excommunication. The world

---

[1]Philip Schaff, *History of the Christian Church*, vol. VIII, chaps. 8–14, 145 (New York: Charles Scribner, 1910).

was changing, but that change had not yet arrived in Noyon or in the Calvin family. John Calvin "received the tonsure," the medieval rite of shaving the crown of one's head that symbolized preparation for the priesthood. Though he would one day be a leader of the Reformation and a religious revolutionary, for now the young John Calvin was proceeding along a very traditional "career track."

Career advancement meant study, something at which John Calvin had proved quite capable from an early age. Since the best education in sixteenth-century France was centered in Paris, John would soon make his way to Paris with his friends, the Montmors.

Exactly when he made this move is the subject of some disagreement. Records are quite obscure. The traditional view (Schaff, Walker, et al.) puts Calvin's move to Paris in August of 1523, at the age of fourteen. More recent scholars (Parker, McGrath, et al.) have opted for an earlier departure, generally in his twelfth year, shortly after receiving the income of his chaplaincy. Regardless of the exact date, Calvin's time in Paris is important not so much for any one thing that he did while there but as the foundation for the mental discipline of his thinking. He mastered Latin in Paris. He was trained in classical forms of logic, grammar, and rhetoric. He encountered the emerging wave of scholarship referred to as "humanism" that sought to return studies to original sources and first foundations.

Owing again to the ambiguity of the sources, it is

difficult to reconstruct the exact picture of this part of John Calvin's life. Calvin was far too reticent himself to leave any descriptions or even many clues. Biographers have been left to work with inferences, general knowledge of the times, recollections of later friends, and the weight of the tradition that would spring up after Calvin's death.

For our part, it seems that Calvin first arrived in Paris by 1521, at the age of twelve, to begin a course of studies comparable to preparatory school. This was probably done at the College de la Marche, one of the many smaller "colleges" that comprised the University of Paris. This was a typical age and circumstance for those pursuing these studies.

This preparatory curriculum was known as the "grammar course." It was designed to equip the student with a thorough working knowledge of Latin, the universal language of scholarship at that time. This was a far-ranging course of studies beginning with basic reading and writing, proceeding through grammar forms and irregularities, and ending with elementary logic from the writings of Aristotle. The primary textbook was the *Doctrinale* by Alexander of Ville-Dieu. Dating back to A.D. 1200, it was still in use after more than one hundred editions! The book presented the student with grammar forms in 2,645 lines of verse that were to be memorized, whether understood or not. Multiply the educational couplet "i before e, except after c, or when followed by g as in 'neighbor' and 'weigh' " thousandfold, and you can begin to understand the size of the student's challenge.

While completing this grammar course, the young Calvin had opportunity to study with Marthurin Cordier, the most outstanding Latin scholar of that day. Cordier produced his own Latin grammar, one that would remain popular and in use until the beginning of the nineteenth century. At this time a Roman Catholic priest, Cordier would one day convert to Protestantism and even seek refuge in Calvin's Geneva, becoming director of the College of Geneva. In 1550 Calvin dedicated his *Commentary on I Thessalonians* to this great Latin teacher and colleague.

> When I was a child, and had merely tasted the rudiments of Latin, my father sent me to Paris. There God's goodness gave you to me for a little while as preceptor, to teach me the true way to learn so that I might continue with greater profit. . . . For me this happy start to the study of Latin happened by the special blessing of God.

From the very beginning, in Paris, John Calvin demonstrated a quick and capable mind. Biographer Theodore Beza records that "he so profited that he left his fellow students in the grammar course behind and was promoted to dialectics and the study of the other so-called arts." With the successful completion of the grammar course, he was able to enroll in the "arts course" of study and formally affiliate with the College of Montigu, University of Paris.

———

A student "war" erupted during Calvin's enrollment in his new place of study. The silly dispute involved the paving of the street that separated the College of Montigu and the College de Sainte-Barbe. The street had for years been a dangerous place of thieves, muggers, and drunks. It was filled with the stench produced by the Montigu sewer system, which emptied onto the road and drained off through the mud.

In an effort to improve life in the area, the Paris City Council had ordered the street paved, with costs divided between the two colleges. When the job was done, the criminal elements remained, as did the sewage, which could no longer seep into the mud. In fact, the slope of the paving actually directed flow of the sewage into the College de Sainte-Barbe. By cover of night, and led by angry faculty, students from Sainte-Barbe began to undo the project, pulling up paving stones. Incomplete by morning, the students resumed their work the next night, only to be interrupted by an attack from the students of Montigu, who had been at work preparing their counterattack all through the day.

The situation was finally resolved, and the street repaved, when Montigu agreed to construct a drain that would direct the open sewage away. Such was university life in Paris at the beginning of the sixteenth century!

The College of Montigu had been founded in 1374. Toward the end of the fifteenth century, the college was reorganized by its principal, Jean Standonck. He had been educated by the Brethren of the Common Life, a minor movement of renewal centered around Gerard Groote, a man of deeply evangelical and mystic piety. Standonck sought to make Montigu a religious college that could be called an educational monastery, aimed to be "a community of poor clerks who, under the most severe rules, were preparing to become priests and 'reformed' monks."

Later Noel Beda was named principal of Montigu. A theologian of some power, Beda epitomized the sharp-minded protector of the status quo. He could be called conservative, but not as one for whom the Scriptures or even the early creeds were alive. He was simply a defender of the current practice. This traditional, ecclesiastical preference was certainly consistent with the direction that Calvin's father intended for his son's education. It is ironic that Calvin the Reformer and revolutionary began his life's journey directed on a very traditional course.

Throughout this era, Montigu played a role in the training of a number of well-known French figures. The great scholar Erasmus had studied there. The sharp-tongued French satirist François Rabelais was very critical of his time at Montigu. It is interesting to note that just after Calvin left the college, a student by the name of Ignatius Loyola began his studies there. Loyola later founded the Jesuit order within the Roman Catholic Church. As Philip Schaff remarks, "The leaders of the two opposite currents in the religious movement of the sixteenth century came very near living under the same roof and sitting at the same table."[2]

Despite an occasional riot, life at Montigu during Calvin's time was fairly ordered and disciplined. A typical day sounds to our modern ears more like a monastery than a university.

> Up at four o'clock for the morning office (prayers), followed by a lecture until six, when Mass was said. After Mass came breakfast, and then, from eight until ten, the *grande classe*, with a discussion for the ensuing hour. Eleven o'clock brought dinner, which was accompanied by readings from the Bible or the life of a saint, and followed by prayers and college notices. At twelve the students were questioned about their morning's work, but from one to two was a rest period with a public reading. Here our sources skip an hour, and it may be that the students were left free until the afternoon class claimed them from three until five. Now vespers were said, and after vespers a discussion on the afternoon class took place. Between supper, with its attendant readings, and bedtime at eight in winter or nine in summer, there was time for further interrogation and for chapel. On two days a week opportunity was given for recreation. Students were permitted to play games or to be taken for a walk in the Pre-aux-clercs, the university recreation ground.[3]

For all its religious trappings, Montigu was not a monastery or seminary for religious training. It was a college of the University of Paris. Its purpose was to

---

[2]Schaff, 145.
[3]Parker, 8.

prepare students for their Bachelor of Arts degree. Its curriculum, as seen in the daily schedule, was centered on logic and disputation, always conducted in Latin.

Books or courses could vary widely from college to college and teacher to teacher, so it is impossible to reconstruct the details of Calvin's actual studies. More than any particular mentor or subject, it was training in the *process* of logical analysis that affected Calvin and prepared him for his future calling. Very little student work was written. The essay or written examination that contemporary students are familiar with was unknown. Examinations were oral. Classes were participatory. Even lectures were followed with interaction. Texts and arguments were analyzed on the spot. Presentations and responses were immediate. Montigu was, for John Calvin, four years of sharpening skills.

Of Calvin's own life and personal development during this time we know almost nothing because he did not keep a diary. Detractors from later years said that Calvin was known as "the accusative case" by his fellow students because of his critical spirit and sharp language skills. Even his associate Beza wrote that, during his student years, Calvin was "a strict censor of all vices among his associates." We have no evidence that he was isolated, unfriendly, or misanthropic by nature. In the words of biographer Williston Walker, Calvin appears to have been "a student of high personal character, great linguistic and dialectic promise, able to make and keep friends whose interest in him must have been primarily due to the attractive qualities of head and heart which he revealed to them."[4]

The College of Montigu would later be repressed during the time of the French Revolution and, shortly thereafter, completely demolished. A small plaque near the original site is one of the few reminders that John Calvin, the Reformer of Geneva, had his academic beginnings in Paris.

---

[4]Williston Walker, *John Calvin: The Organizer of Reformed Protestantism* (New York: Schocken Books, 1906), 43.

3

A New Course of Studies

Sometimes, the more things change, the more they stay the same. So it could be said of John Calvin's life after he completed his arts program in Paris. When he was approximately seventeen years old, he completed the program and advanced to the "Superior Faculty" to work on his Master's degree.

Given the forceful and consistent direction of his father, one would expect John to advance in the study of theology. Instead, he left Paris for the newly reorganized College of Orleans and the study of law. He later wrote in passing that his father saw law as the "surest road to wealth and honors."

What was it that motivated Gerard's change of plans for his son? By 1525, the Reformation in Germany and Switzerland had become a force to be reckoned with. Perhaps the Roman Catholic Church as an institution was looking much less secure for one's future. Gerard himself may have begun to sense his own loss of standing with the cathedral in Noyon. Whatever the reason, it seems that the career-oriented motivations remained the same, and nowhere was there a shred of religious determination.

The move from Paris to this new school was a dramatic change for John. Gone was the "educational monastery" vision of life that permeated Montigu. Rabelais' satires suggest that students at Orleans were more interested in tennis than law. While the outer restraints of Montigu fell away, it only served to display Calvin's own formidable self-discipline and determination.

Orleans was not organized with the collegiate system of Paris. Instead, it had a single faculty focused entirely on law. Of eight professors, five taught Civil Law and three, canon law. This did not mean that the law school at Orleans was "secular" in our modern sense. Law, even Civil Law, was bound to the unifying vision of Christian society that still hung on from medieval times. The Roman Catholic Church was the most pervasive single institution in Europe. It would not be unusual for a student like Calvin to become a priest who specialized in Civil Law for the Church. In fact, in September of 1527, just prior to transferring to Orleans, Calvin had received a second endowed position from the bishop of his hometown. John Calvin began his legal studies very connected to the old order of things.

· The focus on Civil Law at Orleans opened up the intellectual atmosphere at the college. While Paris was conservative, sitting atop its throne as the premier French university, and happy to continue its excellence in the status quo, Orleans was more the upstart. Practically speaking, this meant an openness to the rising tide of academic inquiry known as "humanism." This humanism was quite different than our modern notion. Today, humanism is typically connected with "human-centered" secular or atheistic ideas. In contrast, the humanism of the fifteenth and sixteenth centuries was marked by a flourishing of classical studies and a desire to return to original sources and root ideas.

> Humanism was concerned with *how ideas were obtained and expressed* rather than with the precise nature of the ideas themselves. A humanist might be a Platonist or an Aristotelian—but in both cases, the ideas involved were derived from antiquity. A humanist might be a skeptic or a believer—but both attitudes could be defended from antiquity. The diversity of *ideas*, which is so characteristic of Renaissance humanism, is based upon a general consensus concerning *how those ideas are to be derived and expressed.*[1]

Calvin went to Orleans to study with some of the best legal minds of his day. During this period of history, Francis I was consolidating his rule over France by centralizing the administrative bureaucracy. His chief obstacle was the wide variety of legal practices across the country. The king encouraged schools and teachers to train students in theoretical aspects of general codes of law based on universal principles be-

---

[1] Alister E. McGrath, *A Life of John Calvin: A Study in the Shaping of Western Culture* (Cambridge, Mass.: Blackwell Publishers, Inc., 1990), 54.

cause he wanted a uniform legal framework for his nation.

This new perspective fit perfectly with the general concern of humanism for original, root sources of ideas. Teachers like Guillaume Bude and Pierre d'Estoile helped establish a tradition of French Legal Humanism that skipped past the centuries of local traditions and the voluminous commentaries and glosses on legal texts and appealed directly to the classical legal sources in their original languages.

Calvin would have studied the *Corpus Iuris Civilis*. This text was the product of a far-reaching compilation and editing of all previous Roman law and legal writings that was undertaken during the reign of the Emperor Justinian, between 529 and 534. It was a massive Latin work composed of three distinct parts. The *Codex* was the heart of the *Corpus*, for it was the definitive statement of Roman law. It was followed by the *Digesta*, a historical commentary on the *Codex* arranged by subject. It set out the more important statements by the earlier Roman lawyers to provide a "history of interpretation" perspective on the text. Finally, there was the *Institutiones*, which was designed to be an authoritative textbook for students. Together they provided a detailed and systematic legal curriculum. Calvin studied and learned about every manner of conflict and resolution subject to jurisprudence: the disposal of rainwater, rights of way, leases, purchase and possession, marriage and divorce, and inheritance. Years later, when his ministry in Geneva would involve him in a dizzying array of civic affairs, he was not without preparation, so his decisions and counsel were not as arbitrary as some have insinuated.

By every report Calvin thrived in Orleans. His mastery of Latin coupled with a powerful memory and clear reasoning abilities put him far ahead of his classmates. His preparation and grasp of topics were so complete that he began to regularly substitute for his professors when they were unable to appear in class for a day. During this time, many European universities and scholars were asked for opinions regarding one of the most discussed topics of the day: the divorce of England's Henry VIII. Calvin argued against the king and lawfulness of marriage with a brother's widow.

It was apparently at Orleans that Calvin developed both his keen memory and his ill health. Beza would write:

> Friends with him then, bear witness that it was his habit to take a light supper and work until midnight; when he awoke the next morning he lay for a long time in bed meditating on and so to say digesting what he had read the night before—nor would he lightly allow his meditation to be interrupted. By these continual vigils he attained his substantial learning and preeminent memory, but it is also likely that he brought on that weakness of the stomach that was the cause of his various illnesses and at length of his early death.

Though Calvin had great respect for his professors, in 1529 he and a number of colleagues were drawn to a different law school located in Bourges, France. Bourges was also a new school on the rise. Under the direction of Marguerite d'Angouleme, Bourges had been thoroughly reorganized after the model of Orleans. This Marguerite, sister to King Francis I of France, later became Queen of the Spanish province Navarre through marriage. From that position, she would one day take great interest in the winds of renewed spiritual interest that blew through French Catholicism. Her book *Le miroir de l'ame pecheresse, The Mirror of a Sinful Soul*, presented a view that was more mystic than reformational in outlook. She used her royal position to act as an occasional protector of those with new religious ideals, including some Reformers. In the years that followed, Marguerite found herself the brunt of attacks from the conservative Catholic hierarchy.

Under Marguerite's direction, the College of Bourges had enticed the renowned Italian jurist Andrea Alciati to join the faculty. Alciati was a lawyer of celebrity status and is still recognized as a central figure in the history of law. As both a practicing lawyer and humanist scholar of great skill, he was a mediator between the old legal structures and the new, emerging methods. His arrival in Bourges was met with unprecedented celebration by the entire town.

Unfortunately, Alciati's lectures focused on repeating the traditional material instead of presenting his new methods. Many, John Calvin included, were disappointed. Within eighteen months Calvin returned to Orleans. This brief interlude with Alciati seemed to have had minimal impact on his development. It was indicative of Calvin's thirst for the new humanist thought that he would leave a beloved school for another in an effort to quench this desire for knowledge. Indeed, at the age of twenty-one, Calvin entered a stage of his life in which he appeared to be more of a vagabond professional student than a stolid Reformer.

There was one very significant seed planted while a student at Bourges. Calvin began to study Greek with Melchior Wolmar. The revolutionary impact of Greek language studies on a student's religious ideas is universally recognized. And yet, back then, such study was thought to be "dangerous." Consider this warning from that era: "We are finding now a new language called Greek. We must avoid it at all costs, for this language gives birth to heresies. Especially beware of the New Testament in Greek; it is a book full of thorns and prickles."

Wolmar had been brought to Bourges by the same sort of lucrative enticement that had brought Alciati. A German by birth, Wolmar was publicly supportive of the German Reformation that was growing under Martin Luther. He had studied as well with LeFevre D'Etaples, the well-known and respected French humanist who was a "pre-Reformation" figure in France, like John Hus in Germany or John Wycliffe in England. Though not a reformer himself, Wolmar would have certainly discussed with Calvin the new religious ideas that were gaining circulation. Their relationship was clearly more than a passing one, for years later, in 1546, Calvin would dedicate his *Com-*

mentary on II Corinthians to him, saying:

> One of the most important things that happened
> to me was in those early days when I was sent by my
> father to learn civil law but, under your instigation
> and teaching, with the study of the laws mixed Greek,
> of which you were then professor *summa cum
> laude*. . . . To you it is, however, that I not a little owe
> it that I was at least taught the rudiments; and this
> was afterwards to be a great help to me.

It was during this period that circumstances took
a decided turn for the worse for John Calvin's father
back in Noyon. Gerard had risen to prominence by
serving a particular bishop. This man resigned in
1525, and was replaced by a new candidate who by all
accounts was less than capable. Gerard now found
himself in the service of a bishop who had a position
but no following. As resentment to the new bishop
grew, those in his entourage found themselves under
increasing scrutiny and pressure by local leaders. Records show that on June 27, 1527, Gerard was called
to make an accounting of particular funds that he
managed for the cathedral, similar to the chaplaincies
he had acquired for his sons. This he did not do, and
on May 15, 1528, officials demanded this accounting
and another as well. Reports were never made, and
the situation degenerated until Gerard was excommunicated.

No one has ever regarded Gerard as having a significant personal influence on the life of his son John,
though that lack may be an influence of its own. He

seemed to have been distracted with his life and work when John was young. His support for John and the guidance of his son's career seem driven more by his own goals than by John's best interest. Indeed, John left Noyon for Paris at the age of eleven or twelve only to return "home" infrequently. There is no record of correspondence between John and Gerard in these first twenty years of his life.

It is little more than a footnote to the life of Calvin to mark the death of his father on May 26, 1531. John, studying in Paris at this time, had been in Noyon, presumably during a vacation. His father's illness detained him there until Gerard's passing a few weeks later. Still officially excommunicated, it took the best efforts of his sons, Charles and John, as well as their guarantee of the disputed financial matters, to make possible their father's burial in consecrated soil.

John's brother Charles would also be excommunicated later in 1531. His offense appears to be some judgment of heresy. Charles would die later in 1537 but, with no one to plead his case, suffered an ignominious burial. John Calvin's ties with the city and even the country of his birth had begun to shrivel away.

On February 14, 1532, Calvin is recorded as *licencie-es-lois*, or "licenced in law." He was offered the degree of Doctor of Laws by unanimous decision of the faculty of Orleans, but he did not accept it. Instead, having completed his training and licensing in law, Calvin continued to pursue academic studies. John was free to pursue his life's goals apart from any obligation to his deceased father, and he chose to pursue learning for its own sake. He moved to Paris to begin study in the classics. Now a young man of barely twenty-two, Calvin began work in earnest on his first book.

Three years earlier, in 1529, the renowned humanist scholar Erasmus had published a new edition of the works of the ancient Roman stoic philosopher Seneca (4 B.C.–A.D. 65). In his day, Seneca had been an author of great breadth and renown. It was said that Seneca had corresponded with the apostle Paul. Jerome even referred to him directly as a Christian. It was as the tutor and later advisor of Emperor Nero that he achieved political influence. By collecting his works under one cover, Erasmus encouraged further study of Seneca as part of the swelling humanist tide.

Calvin took an opportunity to publish a commentary on Seneca's work, *De Clementia* or *On Clemency*. This was an early work of Seneca in which he appeals to Nero to exercise clemency "which all men admired in him" as emperor.

Of itself, this commentary would hardly merit mention in the history of classics studies, but it was the first work of John Calvin. Despite being a first work, it shows from beginning to end Calvin's solid and studious nature. One hundred and fifty-six pages in length, it begins with a dedication to Calvin's boyhood friend and fellow student, Claude de Hangest. Next is a short biography of Seneca. Finally, the heart of the work is a careful analysis of Seneca's essay, section by section. The explanatory comments are far-ranging, covering basic historical and exegetical matters as well as issues of language and philosophical importance. Calvin demonstrated a wide range of familiarity with classical authors, drawing citations from seventy-four Latin authors, twenty-two Greek, and seven of the church fathers. It is clear that many of these references came from compilations of quotations rather than from Calvin's own use of the originals. Still, he handled such secondary sources well.

Of particular interest is the fact that the book contains only three references to the Bible, and these in the Latin Vulgate edition rather than the original Greek text. Though no doubt becoming increasingly familiar with the Bible when he wrote of "Christianity, our religion," it still represented a very traditional Catholic understanding. Many have thought that this *Commentary on "De Clementia"* was a subtle appeal to King Francis I, promoting the virtue of clemency on behalf of the emerging bands of Protestants just as persecution of them was about to begin. This seems unlikely. Calvin had not appeared to have settled in his own faith. Such a conclusion is reading the later Reformer into the young humanist scholar.

Though hardly a Reformer, John Calvin clearly experienced one sort of conversion by this time. It was a "conversion" to the new thinking of humanism. As a result of his training in law, the classics and the humanist scholarship of his time created the "engine" that later produced his reforming writings. His life's direction soon changed. Instead of Seneca, he turned his gaze to the Bible. He mastered inductive exegesis, and with this process developed the tools that led him for the rest of his life. He developed his expansive memory, his deductive reasoning, and his ability to synthesize the vast amounts of material generated from that exegesis into a logical and systematic format. Calvin had not yet written *The Institutes*, but the critical skills that were necessary to write it had been clearly established. While John had not yet experienced a saving relationship with Christ, it seems clear that God in His providence had placed the tools that He would use into a vessel that He would soon redeem.

4

What to Do With My Life?

May of 1532 looked like a fresh beginning for John Calvin. Still young, approaching his twenty-third year, he once again pulled up stakes. Paris was a dangerous place to be because of an infestation of plague, so he moved back to Orleans where he could continue his study of law. He carried with him a gift for his friend François Daniel—a Bible, perhaps even the new French translation by LeFevre.

This was the perfect time in John Calvin's life for such a new beginning. With his father gone and details of the estate in the hands of his brother Charles, Calvin had few ties besides the financial support of church appointments to connect with his birthplace of Noyon. In February he had received his *licencie-es-lois* from Orleans. In April his first book, *Commentary on Seneca's "De Clementia"*, was published. The year had been peppered with travel and study, but the time in Paris with Pierre Danes seemed to confirm his yearning for a life of study. This trip to Orleans was not only well-timed, it looked like a suitable career step as well.

Once in Orleans, Calvin apparently continued his study. As a *regent*, similar to a modern teaching assistant, he tried his hand at teaching. Records survive that place Calvin in Orleans and involved in minor affairs of the college through the remainder of 1532 and midway through 1533. By August of 1533, when he appeared before a church meeting in Noyon, Calvin had departed Orleans and returned again to Paris. Now safe from the plague, Paris had become a place of cautious reception for reforming ideas.

The landscape of European politics was changing. The Roman Catholic Church was losing political sway over Germany and England, so King Francis I of France was forced to make his own tentative steps toward reform. This meant he needed to step lightly with regard to the religious reforms of the time in these countries. His own sister Marguerite, now Queen of the Spanish region of Navarre, was openly advocating new religious sentiments in her own book and encouraging a hearing for others with new ideas. She used the king's absence from Paris as her opportunity to promote men like Gerard Roussel and Le-Fevre. Though these men would remain aligned with the Roman Church, their preaching and teaching were far removed from the religious status quo and served the purpose of fanning Reformation flames. Paris was no Wittenberg or Strasbourg, perhaps, but at that time, it was far different from the city of Calvin's undergraduate studies.

Marguerite brought Gerard Roussel to Paris to preach during Lent of 1533. His reform-minded ser-

mons led to an outbreak of hostility from the entrenched traditionalists. The king, interested in promoting the new learning, attempted to quiet matters
by banishing the more vocal of the traditionalists.
Later that fall, another tide of hostility began to rise.
Marguerite and the preacher Roussel, whom she had
long protected, were the object of a satirical play by
students at the College of Navarre. Once again, the
king intervened and forced the faculty to disavow any
intention of condemning Marguerite and her companions.

Calvin arrived in the midst of a city marked by
heightened expectations and tensions. His letters
from these months showed him conversant and interested in the matters at hand. He was on friendly terms
with many of the reform-minded students and teachers and was known to have circulated, with approval,
many of the writings of Roussel. Whether he would
have considered himself a Protestant at this time, or
whether he was simply drawn close by his own involvement in the new learning of humanism, we do
not really know. He did write approvingly of the
events that opened the doors of reform. Indeed, there
was an interest in matters of faith at this time that
was not to be found in his *Commentary on Seneca's "De
Clementia."* He was especially pleased when his good
friend Nicolaus Cop was elected rector of the University of Paris, a position similar to that of the modern
dean.

———

Nicolaus Cop stood tall in the pulpit as the entire academic community of the University of Paris waited for his words. There was an air of tense expectation. It was November 1, 1533. The newly elected rector was to give his inaugural address. More than just a review of institutional affairs and goals or a public relations address, this oration was used by each incoming rector to lay out a vision of life and education that would direct and energize his term. Nicolaus Cop chose for his theme the matter of "Christian philosophy."

John Calvin sat among the listeners with particular interest. As one in a close circle of Cop's friends, Calvin knew exactly what was on Cop's mind and in his address. They had often talked late into the night about matters of life and faith. All of Europe was wrestling with new views of Christian faith. One did not have to be a "Lutheran" or an Anabaptist to sense that there was a new wind blowing through the old institutions of Christian Europe. Though Cop was the one speaking as new rector, it was as if his entire circle of reforming comrades had been elected.

Cop began his oration with a presentation of Christian philosophy that was distinctly Protestant and clearly indebted to Erasmus. Many of the ideas, and even some of the language, can be found in Erasmus' third edition of his Greek New Testament, published in 1524. This Christian philosophy declared that we are children of God.

> To proclaim it, God became man. Those who have

its knowledge exceed other men, as men in general are superior to beasts. It is the worthiest of sciences. It reveals the remission of sins by the mere grace of God. It shows that the Holy Spirit, who sanctifies the heart and guides to life eternal, is promised to all Christians. It gives peace to depressed minds and leads to good and happy living.

Cop's goal for the sermon was that everything spoken might "praise Him (Christ), may savor of Him, may breathe Him, may call Him to mind." These gospel thoughts were closed with a standard salutation to the Virgin Mary, which illustrated the still developing state of reforming ideas in Paris.

If the introduction showed the influence of Erasmus, the main body of Cop's oration was indebted to Martin Luther. A Latin translation of a 1522 All Saints Day sermon by Luther had been in circulation for about eight years. In this sermon, Luther took his text from the Beatitudes of Jesus' Sermon on the Mount (Matthew 5:1–12) and contrasted the Law and the Gospel. Cop demonstrated his debt to the German Reformer by saying, "The Law drives by commands, threatens, urges, promises no good will. The Gospel drives by no threats, does not force by commands, teaches God's utmost goodwill towards us." In his own words, Cop goes on to clearly present the free gift of salvation through grace.

A faithful son may serve his father while the father lives and then receive an inheritance upon the father's death. The inheritance may be seen as a reward of faithful sonship, but it is in no way a debt owed the son by the father. So it is that we may be faithful to God, serving Him and obeying the law as His children. The blessings of God are not the reward of that service. They are instead the benefit of our salvation received by grace.

Cop spent much time on the words of Jesus blessing the peacemaker, saying, "Would that in this our unhappy age we restore peace in the Church by the Word rather than by the sword." He also blasted the "sophists who contend perpetually about trifles to the neglect of 'Christian Philosophy.'"

Cop no doubt intended his address as a clarion call for Protestant ideals as part of the "new learning" that was gaining strength in the University of Paris. Unfortunately, so bold a declaration seemed to cross an unseen line. By taking new religious ideas into the territory of "Lutheranism," Cop was now seen as a threat to the value of the "new learning." He quickly came under attack. His boldness seemed to prove the contentions of the traditionalists so that King Francis I, who was more committed to calm than to new ideas, found reason to oppose the rising Protestant tide. On November 26, Roussel was once again arrested. Cop had already fled Paris, no doubt fearing his own arrest. John Calvin fled Paris as well.

Calvin's connection with Cop's address has been the subject of much speculation. For years after his death, most believed that Calvin had actually written the speech, meaning Calvin himself was by this time a committed Protestant. There even exists among Calvin's papers a copy of the address in his own unmistakable handwriting. It is now more generally considered that this copy is a personal transcription of the address that marked a most memorable moment in Calvin's life. While he probably did not write the address, we can be sure that he was deeply sympathetic with it. These convictions were in turn well enough known at the time that those who came looking for Cop and Roussel also had the name "John Calvin" on their list of revolutionaries to be detained. Calvin fled the reaction against the Protestantism of Cop's address, because he was sufficiently associated with it to be in danger of arrest. What Cop had intended as the next step forward in the pursuit of truth instead became a blasting cap for the dynamite of persecution that would soon follow.

In mid-1534, Calvin had returned to Paris incognito. The city of his early student years was now a dangerous place for him. The home of his friend Estienne de la Forge, a merchant by trade and a Protestant by conviction, was his safe house. It was a place of encouragement where the faith could be openly discussed and the Bible studied, and where he could wait safely. The rise of the Protestant faith had met with resistance, and, ever since Nicolaus Cop's All Saints Day address, it had been actively persecuted.

Calvin had come to Paris to meet with Michael Servetus, who had just published a book that sought to reform the Church. The book approached the subject in a confused, even heretical way, but apparently Servetus was open to dialogue. John Calvin sneaked back into Paris for an appointment with the man, hoping that his powers of persuasion could correct Servetus' mistaken ideas and even enlist him in the service of the truth.

Servetus never kept his appointment. Calvin waited in vain, and soon left for safer surroundings with no prospects of ever seeing Servetus face-to-face. Or so he thought.

On January 29, 1535, some fifteen months after the fateful Protestant declaration by Nicolaus Cop, there was an ominous parade down the streets of Paris. For more than a year, Paris had been tense and disrupted over the Christian faith. With the muffled drumbeat of a solemn processional, King Francis and his three sons followed the archbishop of Paris. The archbishop held aloft the host, the Communion bread they believed to be the body of Jesus Christ. Leading the processional was an image of St. Genevieve, the patron saint of Paris. Behind the king, two by two, walked a seemingly endless line of princes, cardinals, bishops, priests, ambassadors, and every manner of official from the civil government and University of Paris. The king walked from the Louvre to Notre Dame, bareheaded and on foot, holding a torch as a solemn act of repentance, in hopes of atoning for the rise of Protestant ways and insults.

The fate of Protestantism and Protestants in France had been irreparably harmed thirteen weeks earlier on the night of October 18, 1534. On that unsuspecting night, known as the Night of the Placards, buildings, streets, and churches all across France had been posted with tracts. King Francis himself had risen to find one affixed to the door of his bedchamber in Fountainbleau. These strongly worded tracts attacked "the horrible, great, intolerable abuses of the popish Mass." In these tracts, the Mass was described as "a blasphemous denial of the one and all-sufficient sacrifice of Christ; while the pope, with all his brood of cardinals, bishops, priests, and monks are denounced as hypocrites and servants of Antichrist."[1] This was more than the king could stand, no matter what his sister Marguerite thought. One fanatical move identified Protestantism as a dangerous and revolutionary threat to the stability of France as a Christian nation. The king needed to purge this dangerous movement from the city and atone for the unimaginable defilement caused by such insults of the Mass and hierarchy.

The king's public processional ended at the Cathedral of Notre Dame, where a solemn Mass was performed. At the meal that followed, the king declared "that he would not hesitate to behead any one of his own children if found guilty of these new, accursed heresies, and to offer them as a sacrifice to divine justice."[2] To demonstrate his conviction, all gathered watched the burning of six Protestants. The people were slowly raised and lowered into the blaze until the rope that suspended them burned through, dropping them finally into the heart of the fire. Twenty-four Protestants were publicly burned in Paris between

---

[1]Schaff, 152.
[2]Schaff, 153.

November 10, 1534 and May 5, 1535. One of them would be John Calvin's friend, the merchant Estienne de la Forge.

On January 13, 1535, the Sorbonne would petition the king to halt printing presses in order to counter the spread of Protestant ideas. He agreed to that request on February 26. Later, the presses would be opened, but only under the watchful eye of Church censors who were appointed to review all printed material. Persecution of French Protestants, known as Huguenots, continued for another sixty years until Henry IV's Edict of Nantes in 1598 granted a limited freedom of worship to the Huguenots.

5

The Dawning of Conviction: John Calvin's Conversion

In 1523 John Calvin left Noyon for Paris to prepare for a life in the service of the Roman Catholic Church. He was bright and full of potential. By 1535 this young man had cut his ties with the Roman Catholic Church, was recognized as an emerging leader in the Protestant Reformation, and had begun the book that would shape Western civilization through Protestantism for centuries to come. Clearly, a "conversion" had taken place during this time, but how and when?

Unfortunately, the precise moment of John Calvin's conversion is difficult to determine. While anyone can clearly distinguish between the dark of midnight and bright light of noon, it is often difficult to pin down the instant of the dawn, that single point in time where one side is night and the other is day. In the same way, a "moment of conversion" for John Calvin is difficult to fix with precision. Unlike John Wesley, Calvin recorded no single moment in which he felt his heart "strangely warmed."

Scholars have made their case for any of a number of dates and events between 1529 and 1533, the earliest being while he was a law student at Orleans and the latest centered on his friend Nicolaus Cop's address to the University of Paris. Besides the influences that have already been touched upon, what can we know about Calvin's "moment of dawn"?

We know that Calvin himself called it a "sudden conversion," or even better, an "unexpected conversion." He wrote of it in Latin and used the term *subita conversio*. This reference is found in the preface to his *Commentary on the Psalms*, where he writes:

> God drew me from obscure and lowly beginnings and conferred on me that most honorable office of herald and minister of the Gospel. My father had intended me for theology from my early childhood. But when he reflected that the career of the law proved everywhere very lucrative for its practitioners, the prospect suddenly made him change his mind. And so it happened that I was called away from the study of philosophy and set to learning law: although, out of obedience to my father's wishes, I tried my best to work hard, yet God at last turned my course in another direction by the secret rein of his providence. What happened first was that by an unexpected conversion he tamed to teachableness a mind too stubborn for its years—for I was so strongly devoted to the superstitions of the Papacy that nothing less could draw me from such depths of mire. And so this mere

taste of true godliness that I received set me on fire with such a desire to progress that I pursued the rest of my studies more coolly, although I did not give them up altogether. Before a year had slipped by, anybody who longed for purer doctrine kept on coming to learn from me, still a beginner, a raw recruit.

This statement was written nearly twenty-five years after the event of which it speaks and just two years before the final edition of *The Institutes*, when Calvin's theological reflection was attaining its most mature and highly developed stage. Time and mature reflection are certainly powerful lenses and will affect anyone's perception of their experiences. Still, the outlines of an authentic, life-changing encounter with the Gospel of Christ are plain to see.

First, *a turning*. Coming up to the moment of his "unexpected conversion," Calvin can speak of his stubborn mind, superstitions, and plans for his life. Then, having tasted "true godliness," there is a change of life direction that affects his studies and goals. He is "set on fire" and newly teachable. He is a new man.

Second, *God's grace* is at work. Calvin speaks of his conversion and changed life, but all in response to God's own gracious work. It took nothing less than the activity of God to lift him up from the mire of his superstitions. The "rein" might have been hidden to his own eyes, but it was clearly God at work through His providence that brought the young student to this new life.

Third, *his life bears fruit*. One cannot read Calvin

without finding a man who is deeply confident in God and God's calling while being just as deeply unimpressed with himself. When he stands unblinkingly against the crowds and pressures, it is because he is convinced that God has spoken or called him to act, not because there is something special about John Calvin. Years after his conversion, and universally recognized as a Reformation leader, Calvin was amazed that people would come to him, "a raw recruit," for teaching and doctrine. In his mind, only God could bear such fruit. This attitude is the fruit of authentic conversion.

This passage cited above, from the preface to the *Commentary on the Psalms*, is the only reference to any such moment of conversion that we have from Calvin himself. A few other statements of Calvin, found in his many writings, are taken to be references to his own conversion, though they are not directly attributed as such. The most interesting is from his *Reply to Sadolet*. In this tract, in defense of Protestantism, Calvin writes a dialogue between a Protestant minister and "common man of the people," as a device to present the life-changing validity of Protestant doctrine. Though it was not intended to be autobiographical, the speech from the "common man" is considered to be a window into Calvin's heart.

When, however, I had performed all these things (i.e., had sought forgiveness for sin in accordance with the teachings of the Roman Church), though I had some intervals of quiet, I was still far off from true peace of conscience; for, whenever I descended into myself, or raised my mind to Thee, extreme terror seized me—terror which no expiations nor satisfactions could cure. And the more closely I examined myself, the sharper the stings with which my conscience was pricked, so that the only solace that was left to me was to delude myself by obliviousness. Still, as nothing better offered, I continued the course which I had begun, when, lo, a very different form of doctrine started up, not one which led us away from the Christian profession, but one which brought us back to its fountainhead, and, as it were, clearing away the dross, restored it to its original purity. Offended by the novelty, I lent an unwilling ear, and, at first, I confess, strenuously and passionately resisted; (for such is the firmness or effrontery with which it is natural to men to persist in the course which they have once undertaken) it was with the greatest difficulty that I was induced to confess that I had all my life long been in ignorance and error. One thing, in particular, made me averse to those new teachers— viz., reverence for the Church. But when once I opened my ears, and allowed myself to be taught, I perceived that this fear of derogating from the majesty of the Church was groundless. For they reminded me how great the difference is between schism from the Church and studying to correct the faults by which the Church herself was contaminated.

John Calvin preferred to write about God's Word, and very little about himself. As such, we must gain insight into his convictions by looking at passages from his commentaries, especially the most famous text on conversion in the Bible—John 3:1–21—where Nicodemus comes by night to speak with Jesus. Regarding verse 3, "I tell you the truth, no one can see the kingdom of God unless he is born again," Calvin writes:

> No one can be truly united to the church, so as to be counted among the children of God, without having been previously renewed. This shows in concise form what is the beginning of the Christian life, and at the same time teaches us that we are born exiles and utterly alienated from the kingdom of God and that there is a continual opposition between us and God until He makes us altogether different by our being born again.

In verse 6 of John, chapter 3, Jesus says, "Flesh gives birth to flesh, but the Spirit gives birth to spirit. You should not be surprised at my saying, 'You must be born again.'" Calvin comments:

> The only knowledge of God that now remains in human beings is nothing but a source of idolatry and superstition. The judgment we should use in choosing and making distinctions is partly blind and foolish, partly imperfect and confused. All our energy is used up in vain and trifling things, and even our will rushes impetuously and headlong into that which is evil. Thus there is not a drop of uprightness remaining in the whole of our nature. Thus it is obvious that we must be formed by the second birth, in order to be fit for the kingdom of God. The meaning of Christ's words is that we are born carnal from our mother's womb and must be formed anew by the Spirit so that

we may begin to be spiritual.

If the specific timing of John Calvin's moment of dawn has escaped us, we can still recognize his understanding of the full light of the Gospel.

6

Wanderings

Having escaped from Paris shortly after Cop's address in November of 1533, John Calvin would enter a time of wandering and exile until his arrival in Geneva in 1536. There are points along the way of these three years of travel that we know about—Noyon, Orleans, Angouleme, and Pourtiers.

Calvin could hardly picture himself as a Reformer at this stage of his life. He was a trained lawyer with a love of pure scholarship whose convictions were sufficiently Protestant to make him unwelcome in Paris. Just as Israel had a period of wandering in the desert, so the Reformer himself had a period of time between his Egypt in Paris and his Promised Land in Geneva. It was a time of character development and learning, punctuated with extraordinary moments of God's activities and personal decisions.

There was a flurry of papers and shuffling chairs,

then a breathless silence. Every face in the room, save one, seemed to be saying, "Is this young fellow crazy?"

Finally, a voice broke the silence. "Well, Mr. Calvin." The speaker was at a loss for words; not angry, but surprised. "Mr. Calvin, if that is what you want to do, far be it from us to stand in your way."

The date was May 4, 1534. The place was Noyon, France, John Calvin's birthplace. For a few months he had fled Paris, during which time he wandered uncertainly through the outlying regions of France, staying with friends and sympathizers. It was during his stay in Angouleme, in the fabulous library of his friend Louis du Tillet, that Calvin had the kind of peace and quiet that allowed him to study and to take stock of his life.

In the quiet reaches of that library, the studious young man who was not yet twenty-four years old had almost surprised himself with the strength of his convictions. For years now, his study and prayer had led him in his pursuit of God. Along the way, he had been like one who was so focused on the trail in front of him that he missed the changing scenery of his journey. Calvin now realized that God's hand had truly led him into a new land. In that library, he concluded that beyond the shadow of a doubt, he was a Protestant. Quite a discovery for a young man who had for more than a decade been preparing for a life of service to the Roman Catholic Church.

The conclusion was undeniable. He was earnestly convinced that the Scriptures of the Old and New Testament were God's Word and to be obeyed. The Scriptures, not the traditions of the Church, were the final authority for Christian faith. Indeed, many of the daily practices of the Church actually detracted from the Good News that these Scriptures presented: salvation by grace through faith. It was God's grace through faith in Jesus Christ that had brought peace to his heart and fire to his words. John Calvin had not set out to become a "Lutheran" (follower of Luther), but his pursuit of the truth had now clearly led him past the strictures of the Roman Church and into territory that could only be called Protestant.

Calvin discussed his new self-discovery and its many implications with Louis du Tillet during those five months. Louis was the youngest of four brothers in a wealthy and influential family. He served the cathedral in Angouleme, the city of Queen Marguerite of Navarre. With the growing turmoil in Paris, the protective wings of this city were an attraction to many Protestant refugees, including John Calvin. Du Tillet, in turn, used his position to further aid and comfort various Protestants on the run.

John Calvin had known du Tillet since their early student days in Paris. Now their relationship deepened in many ways. They would become close friends for life and, in years to come, traveling companions. Like iron sharpening iron, the two men discussed, considered, and studied together. It was in du Tillet's cathedral library of some 3,000 volumes that Calvin had the first opportunity to acquire "a more extensive and precise knowledge of the early church Fathers."

It could well have been in du Tillet's library that

Calvin worked through the implications of his growing convictions. The ideas that had convinced him over the years in Orleans and Paris were now more than ideas for him. They were the road map to a Savior, God's only Son Jesus Christ. In years to come Calvin would use as his own the emblem of a flaming heart held in an outstretched hand with the motto *Prompte et sincere*, "Promptly and sincerely in the work of God." With that obedience in mind, he had traveled from Angouleme to his native Noyon. There was only one thing he could do.

———

"Yes, Mr. Calvin, if that is what you want to do, I suppose there is nothing that we can do to prevent you." John Calvin had just resigned from his two income-producing benefices with the Roman Church. It came as a shock to the cathedral chapter, the governing board. Many remembered his father who had secured these positions for him. Things had indeed turned sour between the cathedral chapter and both John's father and brother, but everyone agreed such controversies had little to do with John. He had been the chapter's most promising student, like a star scholarship recipient. Some had heard of his Protestant convictions, but opinion was mixed as to how serious they were. John Calvin was no Martin Luther, so why not try to keep his skills and abilities within the fold like so many others?

"How will you support yourself?" asked another voice from around the table. For those who had a liking for the earnest young scholar/lawyer, this was the real question at hand. Had he thought about the financial impact of such a decision? In the brief words that followed, there was no satisfying answer.

"I simply cannot accept money from any institution that I can no longer hold an allegiance to. It is as simple as that."

"His father would roll over in his grave," whispered one old man. Others simply shook their heads at his insistence. If he had simply kept quiet, they thought, this John Calvin could have at least had a secure income for years to come. Still others felt the words came as an insult. These had long since lost any faith in the church that produced their income, but they never hesitated to receive the money.

"Mr. Calvin, as you have requested, we will enter into the record that on this day, May 4, 1534, you have resigned your position and income as chaplain of La Gesine. Now, sir, you may be dismissed. As for the rest of us, let us turn to our next item of business. . . ."

With that John Calvin rose and left the cathedral of Noyon, no longer living and studying at the expense of the Roman Catholic Church. Some considered him impractical, even a fool for giving up the income. Others admired a man for living out his convictions, regardless of the cost.

As strange as it may seem to the modern mind, this arrangement in which a person received money for a church position that required no religious service or activity was very common at the time. It was a system of patronage and endowment that made the accumulation of power and the pursuit of education possible. Calvin's voluntary resignation from the positions was very significant. In a clear and public way, he cut himself off from the Roman Catholic Church. By deliberate choice, and at real cost to himself and his future security, he cut the ties with an institution whose theology he clearly rejected. He was motivated by his own sense of logic and high morals, unwilling to benefit from a system that now repulsed and persecuted him.

It was shortly after his resignation that another person with an identical name, but clearly distinguished, was thrown into jail twice for disrupting worship at the cathedral in Noyon. Many biographers have concluded that this must have been John Calvin the Reformer, growing increasingly vocal about his Protestant convictions and suffering imprisonment for their expression. This same offender shows up at other times and with heinous crimes, while the John Calvin of whom we write was most certainly away from the city. Later detractors—one named Bolsec, in particular—connect this man's sexual crimes with John Calvin the Reformer in an effort to besmirch his good name. Calvin himself mentioned in a letter to a friend that he had never been imprisoned for his convictions, so we see this time in Noyon as a breaking of ties with his long-held appointments and nothing more.

———

"This is a fitting place," thought John Calvin in a moment of quiet reflection. The place was a cool, dark cave just outside the French city of Poitiers. He was there with a number of friends, where, even far from Paris, life was tense for those who could no longer bring themselves to participate in the Roman Catholic Mass. Repelled by the Mass and declared heretics by others, they found themselves hiding in a cave. It was reminiscent of the early Christians in the catacombs of Rome.

Opening his Bible, Calvin began to read from one of the Gospel narratives of the Last Supper.

> While they were eating, Jesus took bread, gave thanks and broke it, and gave it to his disciples, saying, "Take it; this is my body" (Mark 14:22).

After the reading, Calvin could only think with frustration at what this simple Passover meal had become over the centuries. His emotion, expressed through his sharp mind, could not help but denounce the Mass and the way it detracted from the simple promises of Jesus, replacing the all-sufficient sacrifice of Jesus with a never-ending ritual of priestly control. But this time his denunciations were stopped short. *Let the invitation of Jesus establish its own importance,* he thought. *What can my words do that is not better done by the Word of God?*

"Brethren, let us eat the Lord's bread in memory of His death and passion." John Calvin then broke a bit of bread from the simple loaf, giving one to each person gathered there. Finally, he took one for himself. Each remained silent, overwhelmed by the presence of God among them in that cave. In much the same way, the wine was passed from one to the next. Then, after a prayer of thanksgiving, all prayed together in Latin the Lord's Prayer and confessed their faith with the words of the Apostle's Creed. In apostolic simplicity, they communed with God.

The story of Calvin celebrating communion with others in the caves outside Poitiers is an old and moving one. Both the cave and the story are well-known local lore, and the story is held to be authentic by older biographies. Though other more modern scholars may doubt its reliability, we see it as a reasonable reflection of Calvin's faith at this stage of his life: the humanist scholar now an exiled Protestant searching for the roots and original sources of his personal faith.

A third-hand story credits Calvin with these words in a debate over the Mass at the time. Pointing to the Bible, he says with great vigor:

> "There is my Mass," and throwing his cap on the table, lifting his eyes toward heaven, he cried: "Lord, if on the day of judgment Thou rebukest me because I have not been at Mass and have forsaken it, I shall justly say, 'Lord Thou has not commanded it; here is Thy law, here is the Scripture which is the rule that Thou hast given me, in which I could not find any other sacrifice than that which was offered on the altar of the cross.' "[1]

Far from the turmoil of Paris, newly released from both income and relationship with the Roman Church, and still developing in his Protestant convictions, Cal-

---

[1]Walker, 122.

vin returned to the town of his law studies in 1534. It was here in Orleans that John Calvin wrote his first specifically theological work: *Psychopannia*, or *Soul Sleep*.

The idea that the human soul "sleeps without memory, without intelligence, without sensation, from death till the day of judgment, when it will awake from its slumber," is a doctrine known as "soul sleep." It was one of several theological innovations associated at that time with portions of the Anabaptist movement. These radical reformers were typically seen by Roman Catholics and Reformers alike as a threat to true doctrine and order in the church because of their insistence on believer's baptism and democratic church government. Kings, princes, and rulers of all sorts viewed the Anabaptists as anarchists who threatened the secure and ordered life in the church and community.

Tragic incidents in 1525 surrounding Martin Luther and the Peasants Revolt had made the Anabaptist movement something of a "hot potato" that no one wanted to be connected with. The Roman Church tried to blame the Reformers' ideas for the excesses of the Anabaptists, while the Reformers, for their part, worked hard to distance themselves from the Anabaptists. Indeed, just before Calvin wrote *Psychopannia*, a group of Anabaptist prophets took over the town of Münster in the province of Westphalia near the Dutch border and declared the pending dawn of the kingdom of God. Treated as a revolt, the town was forcibly retaken by troops with much loss of life. This incident was surely in Calvin's mind as he wrote his book.

Psychopannia is both a refutation of this doctrine of soul sleep and an argument against the Anabaptists. Calvin apparently sought to distance the mainstream Protestants from the more threatening Anabaptists in the eyes of the French King Francis I. Its importance as a treatise lies not in its impact on Francis I, but in his careful examination of a vast number of Bible passages by which Calvin makes his argument. Though not printed until eight years later in 1542, the work is a first glimpse at the developing exegetical powers of the young scholar.

Here, too, is seen a first glimpse of Calvin the Reformer. In his preface, he writes of a compelling responsibility to write the truth: "If in such need I am silent or dissimulate, I do not see why I should not be called a betrayer of the truth." John Calvin had heard the first whisper of a higher calling.

7

A Rising Star and Wandering Scholar

John Calvin was exhausted and cold, but too relieved to be discouraged, too glad to be done with the past month to be worried about the next one. It was January of 1535. Calvin and his friend Louis du Tillet had left Orleans entirely and now found themselves in a student boardinghouse run by Catherine Klein in Basel, Switzerland.

As the previous year had drawn to a close, religious tensions intensified and spread across France. The Night of the Placards incident in October found French Protestants on the run, away from the persecutions of Paris, and often, like Calvin and his friend, out of the country entirely.

Upon leaving Orleans, the pair made their way through Lorraine and on to the city of Strasbourg. Apparently, even this location did not seem far enough from Paris for safety, so, in the dead of winter, the two decided to find a way through the mountains of Switzerland to the city of Basel, a thoroughly Protestant town. Their friend Nicolaus Cop had settled there earlier in the year.

The trip was tarnished by unexpected danger and betrayal, almost costing the young men their lives. Along the way, one of their traveling servants stole most of their money and one of their two horses. The Swiss Alps were hardly the place to be stranded in winter. Their safe arrival in Basel must have been cause for some relief. Still, Calvin adopted the name Martinus Lucanius to disguise his presence. In addition, the French-speaking community in German-speaking Basel was small and secluded. With no knowledge of German, Calvin was somewhat isolated, but work with friendly faces would mean more security than they had known in France. During this time, Calvin had opportunity to interact with other Protestant scholars like Heinrich Bullinger and Guillaume Farel. Even the aged Erasmus would come to Basel for refuge later in the year.

Shortly after their arrival, Calvin was asked to give editorial assistance to his cousin Pierre Robert, finishing work on a new French language translation of the Bible. Though the two had known of each other growing up in Noyon, it was not until their student days in Paris and Orleans that the cousins developed a deep and mature friendship. Nicknamed *Olivetan*, or "Midnight Oil," Pierre had held Protestant convictions for many years and had fled to Strasbourg in 1528. It may well have been he who first challenged the scholarly Calvin to a more personal commitment.

Now circumstance brought the cousins back together, and they formed a natural team.

Robert had begun the work of translating in 1532 for the French-speaking Waldensians. By June of 1535, the work was completed and published. Calvin contributed two prefaces to this edition. One in Latin begins, "Jean Calvin to all Emperors, Kings, Princes, and Peoples subject to the rule of Christ," the other in French, "To all lovers of Jesus Christ and His Gospel." Though not involved in extensive translation work, Calvin was asked to review and edit the final French text.

It was also in Basel that the first edition of *The Institutes of the Christian Religion* was published. Produced by Basel printers in March of 1536, the work was probably completed before August 23, 1535, the date of the dedication. We can surmise that Calvin had been at work on *The Institutes* even before he arrived in Basel, perhaps back in du Tillet's library in Angouleme.

The Institutes was a near-instant success. Though virtually unknown outside his own circle of friends and colleagues, the strength of this writing would put John Calvin "on the map" of influential Reformation figures. Over the ensuing years, while Calvin was pastoring, teaching, preaching, parenting, and writing, *The Institutes* would be enlarged and go through many editions, though it did not change in substance. With the Basel edition, the die had been cast. It was Shakespeare who wrote, "Some are born great, some achieve greatness, and some have greatness thrust upon them." John Calvin was about to emerge as the man he is immortalized to be, though it would require a bit more travel.

Calvin and du Tillet had left Basel in March of 1536 and set out for Ferrara, located in the Italian Alps. The reason for the change of location is something of a mystery. As a budding young scholar, Calvin may have found employment in the service of Duchess Renee. As a court secretary, he could have used his legal skills, been well supplied, and had ample time to pursue his other interests. This appealed to Calvin, who was still more the retiring scholar than the public figure he would become.

During his short stay in Ferrara, Calvin kept a very low profile. He certainly had opportunity to share his convictions with Duchess Renee and would begin a correspondence with her that would carry on through the years of his ministry.

Calvin probably suspected soon after his arrival that his time in Ferrara would be short. It was hardly a settled place. The Duke, Hercules II, was a devout Roman Catholic and ardent supporter of Charles V, the Holy Roman Emperor. The Duchess Renee, on the other hand, was an ardent French Loyalist, a daughter of King Louis XII, and sister to the wife of Louis' successor, King Francis I. In addition, Renee was a second cousin to Queen Marguerite of Navarre, and deeply affected by her Protestant inclinations. This meant that while the Duke sought to align his court with Charles and the Holy Roman Empire, his wife Renee was working just as hard to resist his efforts by aligning the court with Francis I and France. At the same time, Renee was providing shelter and support for Protestant artists, scholars, and pastors who were equally despised by both kings.

Within weeks of their arrival, a French clergyman who had settled in the Court of Ferrara was arrested and charged with "Lutheranism." By this time most French refugees had probably already departed. Calvin and du Tillet may well have left sometime in April. Calvin would later write that he only entered Italy to leave it.

After their brief sojourn in Ferrara, the two friends parted ways in Basel, du Tillet heading for Neufchatel and Geneva, Calvin returning to Paris to take care of some family business. Changes in the international scene led to a brief lull in King Francis I's persecution of Protestants. Seeking aid from the German princes against Emperor Charles V, King Francis granted six months of free passage to anyone charged with heresy, provided they recant their errors within six months. This was granted in the Edict of Coucy on May 31, 1536, and John Calvin surfaced almost immediately in Paris.

On June 2, he had power of attorney granted to his younger brother, Antoine, who ten days later was in Noyon selling land that had belonged to the family. John apparently stayed in Paris while Antoine handled the business. Upon Antoine's return, the two brothers and their sister Marie were once again on the road, no doubt fearing a future return of the persecutions. John Calvin wanted no more winter traveling. He intended to head for Strasbourg, where the siblings could settle in for a more peaceful and undisturbed life.

Unfortunately, even these plans were altered. The direct route from Paris to Strasbourg was blocked by warring factions. They would need to take a long detour around the hostilities, placing them for a night in the town of Geneva.

8

Geneva and the Thunder of God

M ay God himself be pleased to curse this leisure that you seek for these studies of your
own desires. You have been called to this
great work of the kingdom of God right here in Geneva. If you go through with your plans to turn from
it and leave tomorrow morning, you will never find the
peace that you long for!"

Silence filled the meeting room of the Genevan inn.
Guillaume Farel had spoken his heart. John Calvin
himself seemed overwhelmed. Others in the room, his
brother and sister included, were stunned and wide-
eyed. Calvin's friend, du Tillet, sheepishly sank into a
dark corner. He too had wanted his gifted friend to
stay and work in Geneva, as the Reformation was
slowly taking hold in the bustling Swiss frontier town.
The efforts would clearly benefit from the skills of the
budding young theologian. It was probably du Tillet
who told Farel of Calvin's presence in Geneva, a stay

that was to have been for only one night. It seemed a good idea for the two men to meet, but du Tillet never imagined that the encounter would come to such an explosive head. *God curse his leisure?* du Tillet thought to himself with disbelief. *What have I brought down upon my friend?*

Tall, and with flaming red hair, Farel was twenty years older than the young Calvin. At this moment, he looked for all the world like an Old Testament prophet, or Moses about to smash the Ten Commandment tablets. If Farel had any second thoughts regarding his outburst, he kept them hidden. He was no retiring scholar. Having fled persecution for his faith thirteen years earlier, Farel had since led a band of Protestant evangelists that worked primarily in French-speaking Switzerland. Under his efforts, the influential city of Bern had become thoroughly Protestant. Now Geneva held his prayers and his attention, and John Calvin was the man he wanted for the job.

The silence in the inn held for a time, but for John Calvin's sharp and quick mind, it was long enough to call to mind a couple of recent events: the death, in Paris, of his friend Estienne de la Forge, and his own resignation of the benefices in Noyon. These events swept through his memory on the rising tide of his own conviction, planted through the course of his studies, nurtured by mentors and in the library of his friend, and expressed in his recently finished first draft of the *Institutes*. This was no time for argument or reflection. Calvin would either rise in the morning to continue his journey to Strasbourg or he would rise to set his energies to the reform of the city of Geneva.

"I am not my own," he said quietly. The events and emerging ideas of the past years pointed with a new clarity to a higher calling. There had been an unseen hand at work bringing him to this moment of decision. Having risen slowly to his feet, John Calvin spoke to those around him. "I will stay and work." Years later, John Calvin would record his own reflections on this pivotal evening in July of 1536:

> Guillaume Farel kept me at Geneva, not so much by advice or argument, as by a dreadful curse, as if God had laid his hand upon me from heaven to stop me. . . . And after having heard that I had several private studies for which I wished to keep myself free, and finding that he got nowhere with his requests, he gave vent to an imprecation, that it might please God to curse my leisure and the peace for study that I was looking for, if I went away and refused to give them support and help in a situation of such great need. These words so shocked and moved me, that I gave up the journey I had intended to make.

The sixteenth-century town of Geneva was first established as a Roman settlement on the south end of Lake Geneva in 50 B.C. During the Middle Ages, the growing town served the Burgundian kings as the capital of their region. By the 1000s, Geneva itself was a self-governing city of the Holy Roman Empire. This town and the region around it did not become a part of the Swiss Republic until 1850.

At the time of John Calvin's arrival, the town had

a bustling population of nearly 10,000. Geneva was a commercial town, located just beyond the borders of France, Italy, and Switzerland and, because of that, of interest to all three. The town itself was a fortress, with newly built defensive walls rising like cliffs out of the pastures. Within its secure perimeter, a growing, independent middle class was emerging. By the time of the Reformation, the economy of Geneva had stabilized, even stagnated. More and more, the economic activity of the town was focused simply on housing, feeding, and caring for her own citizens.

While developing commercially, Geneva struggled to establish its identity politically. For centuries, it existed as a vassal city under the influence of the Duke of Savoy. By the sixteenth century, opposing parties had developed within the life of Geneva. One strongly supported the Savoy influence and the other aligned with neighboring Swiss towns in a quest for independence. By the 1530s, the influence of the Swiss faction had grown and included support for the growing Reformation. Evangelists like Farel, Pierre Viret, and Pierre Robert had all spent time in Geneva.

Riots in 1533 reduced the Swiss alliance to Bern alone, rejecting the influence of Catholic Fribourg. Protestant sentiment continued to build. In June of 1535, a month-long public disputation was held between Catholic officials and the growing Protestant factions. By July mob violence had erupted, and the Mass was suspended. Bishops and nuns departed the town.

With this, the Duke of Savoy sought to regain his

control over Geneva by besieging the town. Both Bern and France came to the aid of Geneva with troops. With the Duke of Savoy held off, the town demanded sovereignty: they wanted freedom from both Savoy and Bern. On May 25, 1536, a general assembly of citizens voted to "live by the Gospel." Geneva now joined the emerging ranks of self-identified Protestant towns as an independent republic.

It was about three months after this decision that John Calvin, his brother Antoine, and half sister Marie stopped for the night in Geneva.

Though Calvin stayed in Geneva at this pivotal moment in the development of the town, it is not clear what position he was called to fill. He apparently had no pastoral duties and served as a "reader in the Holy Scriptures" by giving regular expository sermons. This allowed him time to continue working on a French edition of *The Institutes* and to recover from a severe cold that clung to him throughout the fall. In October he was invited to accompany Farel and Pierre Viret to a public disputation in Lausanne. It was to be an eventful moment.

Bern had recently taken control of the city of Lausanne. Anxious to establish the Reformation faith as well as its political oversight, Bern called for a two-week public debate between local Catholic officials and Protestant leaders. These public debates were a common event in the emerging cities of Europe. All the citizens would gather for public presentations and debate on matters of the day, a climate Martin Luther had hoped to create with his famous Ninety-Five Theses. Because Lausanne was a French-speaking town, the German-speaking Bernese asked Farel and Pierre Viret to join them and speak for the Protestant delegation. Calvin was asked to accompany his two friends.

All the prominent citizens of Lausanne listened to the debates for nearly a week. The visiting Protestants made their case, but to little avail. The Catholic clergy of Lausanne argued clearly and with great power and persuasiveness. Everyone was quite surprised and disappointed that Farel and Viret seemed to constantly miss the mark when supporting their Protestant propositions. The Bernese officials were noticeably edgy.

A new round of debates began with the Catholic speaker accusing the Protestants of despising the early church Fathers when it came to understanding the Christian faith: How could these upstarts presume to ignore centuries of faithful men? Were they to believe that men like Bucer, Zwingli, and this babbling Farel knew more than Chrysostom? Would God leave His church in the dark for centuries, only to trust the faith to spring from such unknown sources? Who is to be trusted to understand the words of Scripture? The Fathers that Rome had so carefully guarded these many centuries? Or these Swiss soldiers and lawyers who clearly intended to start a new church for their own political ends?

The statement left the Protestant delegation at a loss for words. After some hesitation, Farel and Viret remained seated. Instead, John Calvin stood to speak in response. Nothing could be further from the truth than these groundless accusations. Though Rome and these Popish priests may have held the books that contained the words of these great and holy Fathers, it was the Protestants who held to the content of their belief! Calvin begged the hearers to consider: Who loves a field more? Some absent prince who holds a deed and sucks revenue from the work of the farmer? Or the farmer who day by day and season by season plants and tills and gives thanks to God for the harvest? The bishops and cardinals become so accustomed to their ownership of the Fathers, that they long since stopped caring for the message the Fathers spoke.

Indeed, it was the Protestants who not only respected the early Fathers of the church by holding to what they wrote, but also knew far better *what* they, in fact, wrote!

Both sides were stunned as Calvin presented each Protestant proposition with careful and extensive reference to the early church Fathers. He presented a remarkable series of references from centuries of writings, all from memory and with great accuracy. Years of training, a heart hungry for God's truth, and those months of study more than two years earlier all came together on October 5 in Lausanne.

The crowd was enraptured by this young man who knew what he was talking about. Point by point, with a simple clarity that carried its own persuasion, he proceeded. In due time, it was clear that the tide of the debate had shifted. Calvin not only established the weight of the Protestant propositions, he undercut the Catholic rebuttals before they were even made. There was no response when he was done.

Though the debate continued for several days, its outcome was a foregone conclusion. The Protestants had won the battle of ideas for the hearts of Lausanne's citizens. The Bernese looked with new respect to the town of Geneva and the Reformation that was occurring there. Farel thanked God, realizing that his new associate possessed far more capability than he had guessed that first night at the inn in Geneva. John Calvin seemed to have surprised himself by his capability. Like an athlete who discovers after long training that he is uniquely suited to excel in a particular event, Calvin found the purpose for which he had been born.

The *Institutes*, published barely six months earlier, had begun to establish Calvin as one of the outstanding Protestant writers of his day. And the Lausanne disputation demonstrated to a number of key leaders the power of his personal presence.

Back in Geneva, Calvin's role was still somewhat undefined. He was very attached to Farel, who found Calvin's sharp mind and attention to detail a great support to his own fiery brashness. As late as August 13, 1537, the Council of Bern distinguished between Farel as "preacher" and Calvin as "reader in the Holy Scriptures." Calvin first began preaching and giving expository lectures without performing the typical array of pastoral duties in a local church. But he was, after a period of time, elected as one of several pastors in Geneva.

The world was shaped by his *Institutes*. His commentaries remain fresh and insightful centuries later. Geneva was organized and reformed to become a city of Protestant refuge and light. But it must be remembered that the things that marked Calvin's legacy were all performed while he served and identified himself as a local church pastor. Baptisms, weddings, funerals—all became part of the work of this one-time professional student. In the decade between 1550 and 1559, for example, Calvin officiated at nearly two hundred and seventy weddings and fifty baptisms. Regular services, pastoral care, and board meetings became part of his daily schedule. His special gifts in teaching and training others kept education at the forefront of his work, but always within the context of pastoral work. All that he would produce would be born not from the ivory tower of academia but from the pulpit and life issues of a struggling community of faith. And there would be some struggles.

Because John Calvin's life and work was so tied up with the life of Geneva, it bears a moment to explain the structure of local government within the city. Calvin was a strong personality, and local power structures were loathe to surrender their privilege. The interaction between a town pastor and officials, sometimes supportive, sometimes struggling, was central to the story.

Though little more than a small town by modern standards, Geneva considered itself a representative republic in terms of government. All male citizens were given the privilege of voting, and this *commune* was reserved for major decisions. In November they met to determine the price of wine and to elect the head of the civil court, and in January to elect the four Syndics. These four Syndics served as leaders of the central administrative body known as the Little Council. Comprising twenty-five men, it met at least three times each week and dealt with ongoing matters of foreign affairs, capital sentences, and control of local money supply. The Little Council was elected each year in February by the Council of 200. This larger administrative body met monthly to discuss important legislation and matters. In 1526 membership on the important Little Council was restricted by law to those born in Geneva. In years to come, as Geneva became flooded with Protestant refugees from around the world, this arrangement tended to make the Little Council traditional and conservative, a center for the status quo and inherited wealth, ripe for confrontation with those committed to new ideas and change.

On January 15, 1537, less than eight months after Geneva's declaration of its Protestant status, Farel and Calvin presented to Geneva's Little Council a series of proposed church reforms called *Articles on the Organization of the Church and Its Worship at Geneva*. The *Articles* are a glimpse into the developing Reformed ideas for church life.

First was the proposal that the Lord's Supper be celebrated each week. This was considered to be more consistent with the intent of the sacrament and the practice of the early church, but a radical departure from the two or three times each year that Communion was celebrated under the Roman Catholic Church. As an act of compromise on account of the "infirmity of the people" under years of papal practice, it was suggested Communion be celebrated monthly at first.

With such regular Communion came the need for a more rigorous practice of church discipline. Qualified overseers in various parts of the town were to report serious sins and indiscretions to the ministers. They, in turn, would seek out the offender for counsel and to encourage their repentance. Only after resisting these attempts at reconciliation could any person be barred from the Lord's Supper. This entire process was meant to bar unprepared and unrepentant people from polluting the sacrament, and was not a matter of political or social sanction. Any person barred from partaking would still be expected to be regular in attendance at the preaching services in hopes that the action of God's Word might win their hearts and they be restored.

In addition, failure to subscribe to the Protestant faith was grounds for excommunication. The previous fall, just after their return from the Lausanne disputation, the Council had been presented with a statement of Protestant faith "which all citizens and inhabitants of Geneva . . . must promise to keep and hold."

A second article of reform included the singing of psalms by the congregation at all services of worship. This act of participation and education was intended to add life to their worship and to teach psalms to people of all ages and classes.

Plans to write up a "brief and simple summary of the Christian faith" were made for the purpose of catechizing (training) children. This was clearly stated as an ancient practice and not some Catholic innovation. Now that the *Confession of Faith* had been written for Geneva, there was a need to make it available to future generations.

Finally, the Reformers asked for revision in the marriage laws of Geneva. This delicate matter was to be handled by a group of civil magistrates and ministers who together would report their ideas and findings back to the Council.

The Council studied the *Articles* with great interest. By the end of the day, all provisions but one were adopted. Communion, rather than monthly, would only be celebrated on a quarterly basis, just as it was in nearby Bern. Later that same day, the Council of 200 met and approved the support of the *Articles* by the Little Council. Indeed, they went further in their reforming zeal by decreeing that during sermon times "neither butchers, nor tripe sellers, nor others, nor secondhand dealers shall stay open beyond the last stroke of the great bell; that those who have idols at home break them up forthwith; that there is to be no singing of idle songs and no playing of games of chance; nor are the pastry cooks to cry their wares during the time of sermon."

Unfortunately, their zeal for legislating turned cold when it came to implementation of the same. In

March both Councils were reminded by the ministers that they had passed the *Articles*. It was not
until April 17 that a procedure for securing a subscription (the act of signing one's name, like a con-
tract) to the *Confession of Faith* by each citizen was
developed. Once again, on July 29, the ministers
were asking the Council of 200 to proceed with their
plans. Subscriptions dragged on into November.
They were to be taken district by district throughout
the town. Many subscribed, but some refused. Indeed, there was not a single statement of subscription in one district where the strongest opponents of
the Reformers lived. A meeting of the Council of 200
on November 26 was tense and indecisive. Harsh
words and accusations were spoken. Confusion
reigned, and, in the end, the subscription was limited and of no consequence.

While the subscription issue was delayed
through the summer and into the fall, two other accusations surfaced against Farel and Calvin that
were to hinder their work. Church reform and political independence had arrived, and such dramatic
events gave France good reason to take an increased
interest in the affairs of this disruptive town on its
border. Since both Farel and Calvin were French,
their allegiance was soon questioned. Indeed, in February of 1538, a French agent made his way to Geneva and sought to negotiate an alliance with Geneva through two prominent men who were well-
known supporters of the Reformers. When word of
this leaked out, mobs gathered at the homes of the

ministers, firing guns and threatening to throw them into the river. In some quarters of Geneva, opposing the Reformers soon became akin to an act of patriotism.

Also, during the fall of 1537, Farel and Calvin found themselves accused of heresy. A former priest by the name of Pierre Caroli had been converted to the Reformed faith in 1534 and made a pastor in a neighboring town. When Pierre Viret, a fellow minister of Calvin in Geneva, reported Caroli to the church authorities of Bern for advocating prayers for the dead, Caroli responded in kind by accusing Farel and Calvin of Arianism. This ancient view held that Jesus, as the Divine Logos, was not eternal, but a being created by and subservient to the Father. It had been declared heretical at the Council of Constantinople in 381. Both Farel and Calvin were called to Bern and made a defense for themselves. They were easily upheld, but the fact of the charges tarnished their reputation for quite some time.

Events continued to go from bad to worse. In February of 1538, four new Syndics were elected. These men advocated the increased influence of the nearby city of Bern in the life of Geneva. Farel and Calvin were inclined to follow their own vision of reforms and resist the influence even of Bern. The Geneva Councils increasingly pressured them to conform to Bernese practices. Calvin referred to the Council in a sermon as "a council of the devil." On Good Friday the Council of 200 asked all ministers to use unleavened bread at Communion on Easter. The ministers made no reply. On Saturday they were ordered to obey or be prevented from preaching. On Easter Sunday the ministers preached but did not celebrate Communion at all. Riots broke out in the city. On Monday the Council of 200 met and ordered Farel and Calvin out of the town as soon as substitutes could be arranged for. On Tuesday they met again and decided not to wait for substitutes. Farel and Calvin were to leave Geneva by Friday.

The two went straight to Bern where they made the case for their mistreatment. Bern was convinced, but not Geneva. The two ministers carried their case to a larger gathering of Reformed churches that was meeting in Zurich. Once again they were vindicated, though the Synod did conclude that much of the problem lay with Calvin's "misplaced vigor" and a lack of tenderheartedness toward "so undisciplined a people" as the citizens of Geneva. Though a delegation was sent to Geneva to seek the restoration of Farel and Calvin, the cause was lost. By June both ministers had given up, gathered their meager possessions, and headed to Basel.

We can only imagine the mixture of relief and disappointment that must have followed his expulsion from Geneva. It was for John Calvin the first major encounter with failure in his life. Still, there was great relief at being released from the pressures and entanglements of life in Geneva. While waiting and wondering in Basel, Calvin would write,

> After that calamity, when my ministry seemed to

me to be disastrous and unsuccessful, I made up my mind never again to enter on any ecclesiastical charge whatever unless the Lord should call me to it by clear and manifest call.[1]

[1]Parker, 67.

9

A Reprieve in Strasbourg

Mr. Calvin, God is certainly not done with you yet!" John Calvin turned away from the table and stared out the small window, pondering the words of Martin Bucer.

"Come to Strasbourg," said Bucer. "There are five hundred French refugees like yourself who are in great need of a shepherd. They are welcome among us, but they feel lost in our German-speaking city. The Reformation is secure in Strasbourg and there will be no city council with which to deal. How long will you stare out the window and read your books? Come to Strasbourg."

August 1538 was a difficult time of reflection for John Calvin. Still smarting from the apparent failures in Geneva, and now alone, as Farel had already left Basel to serve in Neufchatel, the victory of the Lausanne disputation seemed a long distance away. He listened as Martin Bucer, a Reformer in the city of Strasbourg, invited him to the ministry there.

"My friend," Bucer continued, "don't be like Jonah

the prophet who ran from God's call! Come to Strasbourg! It is your place in God's service."

There it was again: that sense of call. Bucer, in a manner less threatening than Farel, seemed to speak to Calvin as the voice of God.

Those same days of late summer were marked by the further sadness of several deaths. Farel's nephew, whom Calvin had cared for in his sickness, and Courauld, a reforming colleague from Geneva, both died suddenly. Pierre Robert, Calvin's cousin, and another fellow Reformer died at this time as well.

Perhaps more painful than the deaths was the desertion of his friend and fellow traveler Louis du Tillet. Without warning, Calvin heard from a mutual friend that du Tillet had returned to France and the Roman Catholic Church. A letter from du Tillet himself questioned whether the new Protestant movement could, in fact, be considered the true church, or just a rash act of schism. In a second letter that arrived just as Calvin was beginning his ministry in Strasbourg, du Tillet wondered if Calvin's banishment from Geneva was not a sign of God's displeasure with the Reformer. It was more than Calvin could stand. He wrote back:

> One of my companions (Courauld) now stands before God to render account for what was our common cause. When we also come there, it will be known which side is guilty of rashness and desertion. It is to God that I appeal from the judgments of all worldly wise men who imagine their word carries enough

weight to condemn us. There the angels of God will bear witness who are the schismatics.

Hesitantly, then, Calvin had gone to Strasbourg. By September he was settled in and ministering, and within months he applied for and received citizenship in the city, something he never did in Geneva.

Calvin and the refugee church in Strasbourg seemed an immediate match. For their part, the people were thankful to have a pastor who shared their language, culture, and experience, and they received both his teaching and his pastoral care with open hearts. There were no factions in this town—Calvin was able to minister to a group of five hundred. The unique circumstance gave him the time and space to develop the one thing that was missing in Geneva—personal relationships with his people.

Each day, and twice on Sunday, Calvin preached from the Scriptures. He was involved in teaching a Protestant catechism to the young, and Communion was celebrated once a month. Principles of church discipline were introduced in such a way as to not alienate the church members. Lively psalm singing was incorporated in their worship. One refugee found his way to Strasbourg and remembered the vibrant worship life of Calvin's French congregation:

> Everyone sings, men and women, and it is a lovely sight. Each has a music book in his hand. . . . For five or six days at the beginning, as I looked on this little company of exiles, I wept, not for sadness but for joy to hear them all singing so heartily, and as they sang

giving thanks to God that he had led them to a place where His name is glorified. No one could imagine what joy there is in singing the praises and wonders of the Lord in the mother tongue as they are sung here.

In Strasbourg, Calvin had his first opportunity to interact with other Reformers more mature than himself and less tempestuous than Farel. Regular contact with the gracious Martin Bucer helped develop a much broader view of God's work among the various streams of the Reformation.

With regard to Communion, Bucer and Calvin came to represent a middle ground between Martin Luther and Ulrich Zwingli. Luther insisted on the physical presence of Christ in the elements. Ulrich Zwingli, the leading Swiss Reformer, held that Communion was only a memorial or remembrance of Christ's death. These two Reformers had met at the Colloquies of Marburg in 1529 amid much contention. By the end of the meetings, their differing positions could not be resolved. As a result, the emerging Reformation was grievously split at one of the central practices of the church: the Lord's Supper.

Calvin's position—that Christ was truly present in the celebration of Communion, but that His presence was spiritual rather than physical—was a mediating perspective. He published *A Small Treatise on the Lord's Supper* that presented his conclusions in a concise and compelling form. It was well-received by theologians and understood by laypeople. Martin Luther was said to have read it and stated that if Calvin had been present to offer this view twelve years earlier at Marburg, the ensuing separation between the Lutherans and Reformed parties would never have been necessary.

Calvin's schedule was filled not only with the pastoral care of his congregation but with a great deal of travel. In 1539 the Holy Roman Emperor Charles V sought to relieve the tension in his far-flung empire by sponsoring a series of consultations regarding religion, called colloquies. These representative gatherings were a common feature of this era, and provided a public forum for airing differences of opinion and seeking, when possible, common ground. Calvin was often involved as a representative both of Strasbourg and the French-speaking Reform movement.

Like a recurrent nightmare, Peter Caroli resurfaced. It seems Caroli had left France and the Roman Catholic Church to return again to the Protestant camp. Unbelievably, Farel welcomed him with open arms. In October of 1539, Caroli traveled to Strasbourg and once again accused Farel and Calvin of holding Arianism heresies. Not sure what to make of such accusations, the Strasbourg ministers asked Calvin to publicly subscribe to a set of propositions that affirmed orthodox faith. Calvin refused on principle and in fury, and with much ill will toward Farel, whom he held responsible for Caroli's presence. He felt his ministry and writings spoke for themselves. Finally, Calvin's friend Martin Bucer was able to resolve the matter, keeping Calvin and sending Caroli on his way.

10

Marriage

At the age of twenty-nine, Calvin began to think about a future spouse. The idea was relatively new to him. After all, he had spent his early years preparing for the Roman Catholic priesthood. After that, his law studies left little time for social affairs. Then there followed his time as a persecuted and wandering Protestant academic and the two years as pastor in Geneva. He had hardly had time or fortune to even *think* about marriage. Besides, by personality, John Calvin was hardly the sort to seek the joys and distractions of marriage and family.

Calvin was never one to speak about his personal life, so it is difficult to determine why he seemed to have changed his mind about marriage. We do know that when he first moved to Strasbourg, he lived for a time in the home of Martin Bucer and his wife, Elizabeth. The Bucers had a vibrant marriage and family life. Their home was called an "inn of righteousness" as they ministered hospitality to Reformers and refugees from around Europe. Martin Bucer urged mar-

riage, with its joys and comforts, on all his ministerial
colleagues. More than once he had spoken specifically
to John Calvin.

Even Calvin's friend Philip Melanchthon, Martin
Luther's right-hand man in the German Reformation,
had by this time been happily married for nineteen
years. His marriage, too, was a source of encouragement and care. The only complaint that Calvin ever
heard on the matter from him was that "my wife always thinks that I am dying of hunger unless I am
stuffed like a sausage."

His new line of thinking was probably reinforced
by the living situation that Calvin moved into after
the Bucer residence. Without the sponsorship of the
churches in Noyon, it was a time marked by pressing
poverty for Calvin. He soon chose to take in boarders,
but found their confusions and demands nearly out-
weighed the additional income. John was able to rent
a large home in Strasbourg. To make ends meet, he
was joined by his brother Antoine, his stepsister
Marie, and several student boarders. It was hardly an
ideal situation for the busy pastor of a growing refugee
church. John's time, finances, and patience were all
put to the test. He wrote, "I can't call a single penny
my own. It is astonishing how money slips away in extraordinary expenses."

So, in his own way, Calvin began to contemplate
marriage. John wrote of his interest to several friends.

Always keep in mind what I seek to find in her, for
I am none of those insane loves who embrace also the

vices of those with whom they are in love, where they are smitten at first sight with a fine figure. This only is the beauty that allures me: if she is chaste, if not too fussy or fastidious, if economical, if patient, if there is hope that she will be interested about my health.

And he was in no hurry! "I shall not belong to those who are accused of attacking Rome, like the Greeks fought Troy, only to be able to take a wife."

In February 1540 the first potential candidate moved into his view. She was a wealthy German woman whose brother was a strong supporter of Calvin. The woman proved unacceptable to John, as she neither knew French nor seemed interested in learning it. Besides, though her financial assets might help his situation, Calvin feared that too much wealth could embarrass the reputation of a poor minister. Even worse, she might be unwilling to live within the reduced means that marriage to him would mean.

Calvin's friend Farel had the second candidate. This woman spoke French and was committed to the Protestant cause. She was also fifteen years *older* than Calvin. He never returned the letter.

When a third opportunity fell through, Calvin seemed to despair of ever finding a wife. "I have not found a wife and frequently hesitate as to whether I ought anymore to seek one," he wrote to Farel.

————

"Have you ever considered Idelette?" asked Martin Bucer.

"Idelette!" mused Calvin. "The recently widowed wife of my friend Jean Stordeur? Could there really be such a wife for me?"

John Calvin first met Idelette Stordeur and her husband, Jean, in 1537 while he was a pastor in Geneva. Jean was a committed Anabaptist and had come for a public disputation to present his views of church life and faith according to the Bible. He was soundly defeated in the public debate by Calvin and ordered to leave the town.

When Calvin arrived in Strasbourg, they crossed paths once again. The Stordeur family had found refuge in Strasbourg and were settled there. A friendship between John and Jean developed. No doubt the two men continued their debate, spending time talking and searching the Scriptures together. Soon Jean and Idelette were in Calvin's church each Sunday. Before long, they had been completely won over to Calvin's Reformed views of the Bible's teaching. They participated in Communion, had their son baptized by Calvin, and eventually joined his congregation.

It was a plague in 1540 that took Jean Stordeur's life. Idelette grieved for a husband, and John felt the loss of a friend. Martin Bucer, though, saw the opportunity for a match.

Idelette was an attractive woman with two young children. Intelligent and cultured, she was from an upper-middle-class background of firm religious conviction. Her own father was deprived of his property and banished because of his views in 1533, the fateful year of Nicolaus Cop's address in Paris. Idelette's personal faith had grown to be firm and mature. She and her husband Jean had studied Scripture, thought and prayed deeply about God's purposes, and lived in accordance with their convictions.

Idelette and John were married in August of 1540, with Farel performing the ceremony. Almost immediately they were both struck with illness and were too sick to rise from bed. John would write a friend, saying, "As if it had been so ordered that our wedlock might not be overjoyous, the Lord thus thwarted our joy by moderating it."

This was followed by the demands of the emerging Reformation. John was regularly called away from Strasbourg for conferences and colloquies. Emperor Charles, the ruler of the Holy Roman Empire, was doing all in his power to resolve differences between the Roman Catholic Church and the emerging Protestant churches. The King was feeling hard pressed by Moslem Turks to the east and wanted to present a united front. John no sooner got back to Strasbourg and cared for the pressing needs of the French refugee congregation than he was once again called away. He was gone thirty-two of the first forty-five weeks of their marriage.

Idelette, for her part, was left to move in and manage Calvin's boardinghouse living arrangements. This she apparently did with some success, even at one time finding safe haven for the family away from Strasbourg when the plague hit in John's absence. She was a noble woman of quiet force and dignity.

Near their first anniversary, John received an invitation to return to Geneva to pastor the church and implement reforms there. It was hardly a place with fond memories, yet John felt compelled to investigate the call. In September John made the journey to the town that just a few years earlier had banished him. Finding an open door of opportunity and a friendly reception, he committed to Geneva. The Council promptly dispatched a herald and two-horse carriage to bring Idelette, the children, and what household effects they shared back to Geneva. For Idelette, the move meant leaving her brother and friends behind in Strasbourg for the challenges of this new ministry.

The house at number 11 Rue de Chanoines was provided and furnished for the Calvin family by the city of Geneva. To Idelette, it must have been a welcome improvement to the Strasbourg boardinghouse. Located near the cathedral, the house included space enough for a vegetable garden and a view of the lake. The small garden was planted each spring with herbs and flowers as well as vegetables for the table. Calvin often pointed it out to friends who visited as an example of his wife's hard work and household care.

Life in the new city was hardly idyllic. In 1542, their first summer in Geneva, Idelette gave birth to a premature son, Jacques, who died two weeks later. Both parents were heartbroken. "The Lord has certainly inflicted a bitter wound in the death of our infant son," John wrote, "but He is himself a father and knows what is good for His children." Tragic deaths continued to rob them of children. Three years later a daughter died at birth, and in 1547 another child was delivered prematurely and did not live.

Meanwhile, enemies, who would name their dog "Calvin," would not let their insults and attacks stop with John. His detractors were quick to point to these tragedies as God's hand of judgment on their life. In addition, some discovered that Idelette's first marriage had never been recognized by a civil ceremony. The Anabaptist convictions held by her and her first husband, Jean, taught marriage to be a sacred ceremony of the church and not under the legal jurisdiction of the government. Gossips spoke of her as a woman of ill repute with previous children born out of wedlock.

Eight years after their arrival in Geneva, Idelette succumbed to years of ill health, probably tuberculosis, and she passed away. On her deathbed, her chief concerns were that her long illness did not hinder John's ministry and that her children be provided for. John recounted the closing days of her life in a letter:

> Since I feared that these personal worries might aggravate her illness, I took an opportunity, three days before her death, to tell her that I would not fail to fulfill my responsibilities to her children. She immediately responded by saying, "I have already entrusted them to God." When I said that this did not relieve me of my responsibility to care for them, she answered, "I know that you would not neglect that which you know has been entrusted to God."

Calvin was faithful to his word. He raised the two children, even through much heartache, as his own. Continuing his letter of April 2, 1549, to his friend

Farel, John recorded his wife's final moments:

> About the sixth hour of the day, on which she
> yielded up her soul to the Lord, our brother Bour-
> gouin addressed some pious words to her, and while
> he was doing so, she spoke aloud, so that all saw that
> her heart was raised far above the world. For these
> were her words: "O glorious resurrection! O God of
> Abraham and of all our fathers, in thee have the
> faithful trusted during so many past ages, and none
> of them have trusted in vain. I also will hope." These
> short sentences were rather ejaculated than dis-
> tinctly spoken. This did not come from the sugges-
> tions of others, but from her own reflections, so that
> she made it obvious in few words what were her own
> meditations. I had to go at six o'clock. Having been
> removed to another apartment after seven, she im-
> mediately began to decline. When she felt her voice
> suddenly failing her, she said, "Let us pray; let us
> pray. All pray for me." I had now returned. She was
> unable to speak, and her mind seemed to be troubled.
> I, having spoken a few words about the love of Christ,
> the hope of eternal life, concerning our married life,
> and her departure, engaged in prayer. In full posses-
> sion of her mind, she both heard the prayer, and at-
> tended to it. Before eight she expired, so calmly that
> those present could scarcely distinguish between her
> life and her death.

John Calvin wrote far less about his marriage and
life with Idelette than we would wish. His natural ret-
icence, coupled with the short duration of their marriage and the demands and preoccupations of the Reformation, leave the actual record short. Though John

would write very little of her or her impact on his life and work, we should not assume that there was no life or love between them. When it came to writing about life, family, and personal matters, John Calvin was very private and very reluctant. What record there is points to his deep grief at Idelette's loss and singular devotion to her. He would pay attention to the needs of her children for the remaining fifteen years of his own life. Though he was only forty years old when she died, he would never marry again.

Just days after her death, he wrote his friend Viret, saying,

> Although the death of my wife has been exceedingly painful to me, yet I subdue my grief as well as I can. Friends also are earnest in their duty to me. . . . Had not a powerful self-control, therefore, been vouchsafed to me, I could not have borne up so long. And truly mine is no common source of grief. I have been bereaved of the best companion of my life, of one who, had it been so ordered, would not only have been the willing sharer of my exile and poverty but even of my death. During her life she was the faithful helper of my ministry.

In the years that followed, John Calvin faced the controversies of Jerome Bolsec and Michael Servetus without the support and comfort of his wife. His crowning achievement, *The Institutes*, came to its final form ten years after her passing. Their marriage, for whatever it may have appeared to lack by modern expressions of romance and passion, was rooted in a mutual passion for God's kingdom. Their life together, with its joys and sorrows, was built on a shared sense of God's calling and purposes that were bigger and more important than their own pleasure and self-discovery. Convictions, not convenience, ordered their homelife. In the tight fabric of Calvin's life and ideas, his marriage to Idelette provided many important, though often overlooked, strands.

11

The Ministry of Writing: "A Catechism by Some Frenchman or Other..."

God be praised, thought Monsieur Vadian to himself. *Each of these books should help the cause of God's kingdom.* Vadian, burgomaster and chief Reformer of the eastern Swiss city of St. Gallen, was reading through a March 28, 1536, letter from Marcus Bersius, a printer in the nearby town of Basel. In the letter, Bersius reviewed a long and impressive list of new books that he was printing: church Fathers, Bible commentaries, and classical literature. Included in the list is the mention of "a catechism by some Frenchman or other, dedicated to the king of France." This "catechism" was the first edition of *The Institutes of the Christian Religion*, and the Frenchman was John Calvin! Hardly a sterling review for what would become one of the most influential literary works in Western civilization.

That the printer would see this first edition of *The*

Institutes as a catechism is understandable. It contained only 516 small-format pages organized into six chapters. Modeled after Luther's Lesser Catechism of 1529, the first four chapters were expositions of the Ten Commandments, the Apostle's Creed, the Lord's Prayer, and the sacraments. Chapters 5 and 6 were more polemic in nature and focused on false sacraments and Christian liberty.

"The sum of sacred doctrine is contained almost entirely in these two parts: the knowledge of God and of ourselves." For John Clavin, the proper task of theology lies not in abstract conjecture on Divinity, but with reflection on God as He has revealed himself in relationship with humanity, and humankind in light of that relationship. This first quoted line of *The Institutes* was later developed into several chapters. For now, it demonstrates the kind of pregnant insight that runs throughout this first edition.

Calvin had a definite audience in mind as he wrote during the winter of 1534–35. In the preface, entitled *Letter to King Francis*, the young scholar, not even twenty-eight years old at the time, made it plain that he clearly intended his work to be a defense of the rising tide of French Protestantism. Things were not going well for the movement of Reform in France. King Francis had reacted vehemently to the Night of the Placards, and Calvin's friend from Paris, merchant Estienne de la Forge, had been martyred. When German princes—who were increasingly aligned with Lutheranism—raised a protest, Francis was quick to speak respectfully of the German Protestants while painting a scurrilous picture of the rebellious French Reformers. A clear, reasonable presentation of French Protestant beliefs was needed, one that would serve as both *apologia* to detractors and encouragement to adherents.

The first edition of *The Institutes* was so well received that a new one was soon demanded. The second volume, published in 1539 and again in the scholarly language Latin, grew to three times the size—seventeen chapters. Two new chapters dealing with the knowledge of God and the knowledge of human nature were added, as well as material on the Trinity, the relation of the Old and New Testaments, justification by faith, and the nature of the Christian life.

This edition was forged in the furnace of Calvin's first years in Geneva. The writing was the fruit of his first experience as a pastor, his regular preaching, and his disheartening expulsion from Geneva. The finishing touches were probably made as he became involved in the controversy with Cardinal Sadolet. Completed and printed in Strasbourg, *The Institutes* was no longer a primer of Protestant belief. Rather, it had begun to take shape as a definitive statement of Christian faith as found in the Bible. "My object in this work," he wrote in the preface, "is to so prepare and train students of sacred theology for the study of the Word of God that they might have an easy access into it, and be able to proceed in it without hindrance."[1]

In 1541, as Calvin was returning to Geneva from

---

[1]Quoted in McGrath, 137.

his period of exile in Strasbourg, a French edition of *The Institutes* was published. More than just a translation of the Latin editions, this French work showed several alterations designed to make it more readable among the French population. French proverbs were added as illustrations, and points of interest only to scholars, such as Greek words and references to Aristotle, were dropped.

The Institutes continued to grow as the years passed. In 1543 another Latin edition was released. This included a major new section on the doctrine of the church. Two chapters on vows and human traditions were added, and the material relating to angels was gathered into a separate chapter.

Demand for the book and increasing refinement produced more editions in following years. The *Institutes* passed through nine more editions, until 1559, when Calvin thoroughly revised his work. This edition, printed in Geneva by Robert Estienne, marked the appearance of *The Institutes* in the form now recognized by the modern reader. The material was arranged in four "books," following the order of the earliest and most universally recognized expression of faith, the Apostle's Creed. The first dealt with God the Father, the Creator, Sustainer, and Sovereign King of the universe. The second focused on the Son, Jesus, and the whole truth of redemption. The Holy Spirit was the central theme of the third book, and the fourth dealt with the church, including its relation to civil government. Grown now to five times the size of the first edition, it had eighty chapters, each carefully subdivided with explanatory headings. "I was never satisfied," he wrote in the preface, "until it was arranged in the order in which it is now published." It is a work of majestic scope, clearly organized and cogently presented.

John Calvin did not sit down to write *The Institutes* because he had new ideas regarding Christianity. Indeed, in his mind, he was simply presenting the whole message of the Bible in a systematic and balanced manner. This historic message had remained intact for centuries, until changes—changes that he would have considered corruptions—were made by the institution that had emerged as the Roman Catholic Church. The heart of the Reformation perspective was a return to the original message of the Gospel.

The Institutes has an enduring place in the life of the church because of its clarity of thought, orderly presentation, and comprehensive scope. It stands as the pinnacle of systematic theological expression from the Protestant Reformation in Europe. On one side are the early reformers: Luther, Zwingli, Farel, and Bucer, who were energetic, brilliant men used of God to initiate a mighty renewal of His church. They were pioneers and never had the situation nor the inclination to clearly and systematically develop an expression of their faith. Following Calvin came the "settlers" and a time of more rigid and scholastic Protestant writers: Melanchthon, Beza, et al. Calvin and *The Institutes* stand between these two groups as the lofty peak, combining the ardor of the first with the order of the second in a way that outshines each.

Though Calvin quoted widely from classical literature and the early church Fathers—in particular, Augustine—*The Institutes* drew its inspiration from the Scriptures. The Bible was the authoritative record of God's dealings with the universe and humanity. In the words of historian Kenneth Scott Latourette, *The Institutes* "set forth the entire cosmic drama of Creation, sin, and redemption under the sovereign will of God as Calvin believed that it was taught in the Scriptures. . . . Here was a comprehensive statement of what Calvin believed about God, Christ, the nature of man, immortality, sin, redemption, the manner in which God's grace works in the lives of men, the Church, and the relations of Church and state."

In addition, *The Institutes* was a positive presentation of faith. Calvin often refuted Roman Catholic theological positions and even those of Protestants with whom he disagreed. It was never simply idle argument to win a point of disagreement. His intention was to present true Christianity and to point out error in an effort to clarify truth.

By the end of the century the *Institutes* had gone through fifty-two separate editions, published in seven different European languages, including English in 1561 and German in 1572. While twenty-three years brought new editions and expanded material, it is most notable how consistent *The Institutes* remained.

With all the changes made in the structure of *The Institutes*, very few sentences of the 1536 text, or any intervening edition, are omitted in that of 1559. If sentences are changed, it is for clarification and not to mark a change of opinion. Unlike most theologians, Calvin in a quarter of a century did not revise his position with regard to any doctrine of substance or retract anything he had written. What was added was consistent with what had been stated before and seemed a natural continuation of it. "In the doctrine which he taught at the beginning," wrote Beza, his associate and successor, "he remained firm to the end."[2]

The Institutes is the real source of Calvin's legacy through the centuries. His extensive commentaries continue to be insightful and timeless in quality. He maintained an extensive correspondence throughout the growing community of Reformation leaders. Geneva, under his pastorate, shaped many lives that would one day return to influence their own countries. Still, it is *The Institutes* that comes to mind when John Calvin is considered.

Sometimes the influence in its second or third generation is different from what could have been imagined by the author. The "Five Point Calvinism" of the Synod of Dort in 1619 may have reduced *The Institutes* to a formula, but the relationship is clear. From Geneva to Scotland to the American colonies, the ideas on church and civil government found in *The Institutes* were profoundly important. When Max Weber wrote about the "Protestant Work Ethic" in 1905, he

---

[2]John T. McNeill, *The History and Character of Calvinism* (New York: Oxford University Press, 1962), xiii.

was referring to the impact of *The Institutes* born out over centuries.

Commentaries

"You are letting the devil divert you to other tasks when you should be writing commentaries." John Calvin pondered the words in a letter from his friend Valeran Poullain. The statement had the sting of truth. Even more, it gave a focus to what was certainly a growing inner conviction.

A fresh discovery of the meaning and application of the Bible was central to the growing Reformation movement. Though Calvin's life was filled with a wide variety of demands and pastoral concerns, most of his public time was spent sermonizing and teaching the Bible. Written commentaries could give the material of his sermons and Bible lectures to a far wider audience. *The Institutes*, already well received, were meant to be a summation of what the Bible taught and a guide to its reading. Commentaries would present the foundations of his own study, reading, and method. These commentaries on the Scriptures would be another of the enduring legacies of John Calvin. He published his first Bible commentary, the *Commentary on Romans*, in 1540, while in Strasbourg. In the preface he wrote, "I think I have so embraced the sum of religion in all its parts and arranged it systematically that if anyone grasps it aright he will have no difficulty in deciding what he ought principally to seek in Scripture and to what end he should refer everything in it."

Romans was well received, but with his return to Geneva, additional commentaries were put on hold. Years went by without anything new. With the progress of reform in Geneva, the popularity of *Romans*, and Calvin's growing reputation, demand for further work began to rise. In 1546 a second commentary, *II Corinthians*, was published. From that point on John Calvin wrote or had his lectures transcribed to produce a steady flow of new commentaries. By the time of his death, he had published works on every book of the Bible except Revelation.

If one had to pick the two brightest stars from this constellation of commentaries, they would be *Romans* and *Psalms*. John Calvin had a deep affinity for both Paul and David. This was due in part to the influence of their writings on him. It was also because he could see his own spiritual biography in the lives of these two men.

The trials and conflicts of his own life helped him read deeply into the Psalms. In his prefatory remarks, Calvin said that the Psalms was "an anatomy of all the parts of the soul; for there is not an emotion of which anyone can be conscious that is not here represented as in a mirror. Or, rather, the Holy Spirit has here drawn to the life the griefs, the sorrows, the fears, the doubts, the hopes, the cares, the perplexities; in short, all the distracting emotions with which the minds of men are wont to be agitated."

The Commentary on Romans was the fruit of lectures that John Calvin had given on that book in 1536–1537 during his first time in Geneva. With his strict adherence to method, it sets the pattern for all the commentaries that would follow. An initial statement of the book's theme is followed by careful thought-by-thought analysis. Chapter and verse markings had not yet been added to the text of the Bible as we see it today. As a result, Calvin divided the text into convenient paragraphs and passages of thought for comment. Each section started with his own literal Latin translation from the Greek or Hebrew. Calvin's early training as a humanist scholar always drew him back to the most original source as the most authoritative.

With a text and translation to work with, Calvin then began the task of "exegesis." This careful process of analysis and interpretation is meant to enable an understanding of what the text *said* in its original setting and what it *meant* to its original readers. These steps were carefully taken, for only then would Calvin begin his "exposition" of the text, where he would *apply* the meaning of the text to the life and times of himself and his readers.

This was the beginning of what we now call the "grammatico-historical method." Gone are early allegories that looked for a "meaning" beneath the statements of the text. Medieval summaries of other commentators that barely mention the words of Scripture were not accepted. The Reformers, and Calvin above all, looked to the plain meaning of the text itself. For them, the Bible was not a mystical book of hidden meanings that only special people could know and pass on. It was God's message to humanity.

Biographer T. H. L. Parker summarized Calvin's method of exegesis and understanding of the Bible's inspiration:

> His greatest quality as a commentator was his self-disciplined subordination to the text. The technical studies were merely a means to this end. Yet to say that he let the text speak to him would be trite and misleading. Rather, he conducted a continual enquiry between the detail and the wider context. The attention to the context saved his lexicography (word studies) from becoming static, from imposing what we may call an invariable dictionary meaning onto words. But he did not simply listen to the voice of the Bible. As he listened to the context, he questioned the immediate text; as he listened to the immediate text he questioned the context. It was by this continual process of hearing and of asking on the basis of what he had heard that Calvin was able to arrive in the remarkable way that he did at the "mind" of the author.

Calvin did not, however, write commentaries in order that he might inform the sixteenth century about religion among the ancient Semites of the first century A.D. The Bible is God's Word to man. This means not simply that the writers transmit a message that they received from God, but that in it God himself speaks as really as if he were speaking with his own mouth. Calvin's doctrine of the Scriptures contains some puzzling features; to attempt to harmonize them would be to distort. The main points in it, however, are these: (1) Scripture is the record of God's self-revelation to men; (2) it is also the interpretation of that self-revelation; (3) the record itself

is made at the instigation of God; (4) the interpretation is God's own interpretation of the recorded
events; (5) the language of the record is given to the
writer by God. In this sense the Bible is God's Word
to men, in which he reveals the relationship with
them that he has determined and established in
Jesus Christ, the relationship of Creator-creature, of
Redeemer-redeemed.

God's Word to men is the Bible. God does not address men in a direct encounter of Divinity with humanity, but by means of creatures, creaturely events,
creaturely communication. The Bible is a collection of
documents recording the history of God's relation
with men, and therefore is such a creaturely communication. In that they are documents they are to
be studied and understood only by the methods in
which any documents are studied and understood.
The creatureliness of the Bible is no hindrance to
hearing God's Word but rather the completely necessary condition. Thus the Scriptures are at one and
the same time both God's speech to men in the
thorough-going sense given above and also a collection of human writings which therefore betray idio-
syncracies of literary style, even some inaccuracies
and imprecisions. Calvin saw no inconsistency between saying that "the apostles were the amanuenses
(secretaries or 'takers-of-dictation') of the Holy
Spirit" and finding in the apostles' writings literary
weaknesses or geographical or historical errors; for,
according to Calvin's concept of accommodation, God
genuinely speaks to man in such a way that he is com-
prehensible to him. Within the Divine Trinity, the in-
tercommunication is in the spiritual language of Di-

vinity. Man does not understand that language, but speaks Hebrew, Greek, Aramaic. And thus God in his kindness, says Calvin, speaks to man in the language that he understands, like a mother using baby talk to her infant.[3]

The commentaries, as seen in the appendix of his chronological writings, represent prodigious output by any standard. Once Calvin set to work, commentaries began to flow with amazing speed. This was aided by his regular time spent teaching and preaching from the Bible. Many commentaries, mostly on books from the Old Testament, as well as the sermons that we have, were committed to writing by way of student transcriptions that Calvin oversaw. Jean Crispin, a printer, explained in a preface how this was accomplished.

> In copying they followed this plan. Each had his paper ready in the most convenient form, and each separately wrote down with the greatest speed. If some word escaped the one (which sometimes happened, especially on disputed points and on those parts that were delivered with some fervor) it was taken down by another. . . . Immediately after the lecture, de Jonviller took the papers of the other two, placed them before him, consulted his own, and, comparing them all, dictated to someone else to copy down what they had written down hastily. At the end he read it all through so as to be able to read it back to M. Calvin at home the following day. When any lit-

---

[3]T. H. L. Parker, *John Calvin: A Biography* (London: J. M. Dent & Sons, Ltd., 1975), 76–77.

tle word was missing, it was added; or if anything seemed insufficiently explained it was easily made clearer.[4]

The Institutes and the commentaries are the fruit of one life. They are best understood in light of each other. Together, they shed great light on the life and thinking of one man and his times. If *The Institutes* is the comprehensive and systematic summary of the Scriptures' teaching, then the commentaries, taken as a whole, are the detailed foundational work. *The Institutes* takes up four inches on a library shelf. The commentaries cover almost four feet. John Calvin was no speculative theologian. In *The Institutes* and his many commentaries, he gave definition to the role of a biblical theologian.

Letters

Theodore Beza, Calvin's successor, disciple, and early biographer, wrote of another controversy that was full of animosity:

> Another evil, of a more dangerous kind, arose in the year 1539, and was at once extinguished by the diligence of Calvin. The bishop of Carpentras, at that time, was James Sadolet, a man of great eloquence, but he perverted it chiefly in suppressing the light of truth. He had been appointed a cardinal for no other reason than in order that his moral respectability might serve to put a kind of gloss on false religion.

---

[4]Parker, 129–130.

Observing his opportunity in the circumstances which had occurred, and thinking that he would easily ensnare the flock when deprived of its distinguished pastors, he sent, under the pretext of neighborhood, a letter to his so-styled, "most Beloved Senate, Council, and People of Geneva," emitting nothing which might tend to bring them both into the lap of the Romish Harlot.

With Farel and Calvin recently banished, the religious reforms begun in Geneva seemed derailed, leaving the orphaned church ripe for return to the Roman fold. Roman bishops and cardinals in the area recognized this and looked for ways to reassert their influence. They found several allies inside Geneva, lead by Jean Phillipe, the man who had led the opposition to Calvin the previous year. With the newly installed cardinal Joseph Sadolet, the opportunity seemed right.

Cardinal Sadolet was a man of high moral character, great eloquence, and genuine respectability. He was the ideal candidate to formulate a letter to all of Geneva, inviting them to keep their political independence while returning to the Roman Church. This he did in the spring of 1539.

The Little Council received Sadolet's letter and acknowledged its receipt on March 27. They promised a response to his requests "in due time." Sadolet presented an idealized Roman Church and an invitation to security in the antiquity, universality, unity, and inerrancy of Rome. He cast suspicion on the motives and character of the Reformers. With flourish, he challenged the citizens of Geneva "whether it be more expedient for your salvation to believe and follow what the Catholic Church has approved with general consent for more than 1,500 years, or innovations introduced within these 25 years by crafty men."

Because the letter was in Latin, it escaped wide circulation among the citizens of Geneva, minimizing its initial impact. For those who saw it, Sadolet's letter was troubling indeed. Behind its warm invitation to return to the Roman Church, most sensed the waiting domination of the Catholic Duke of Savoy. Worst of all, they felt there was no one in Geneva capable of a response.

Calvin soon received a copy of the letter in Strasbourg, and within six days had left behind any lingering hurt with Geneva and written a response that was twice as long. It has been called "a masterpiece of the lawyer's art, a defense which is an indictment of the prosecution."[5] In *Reply to Cardinal Sadolet*, Calvin answers his opponent's letter point by point. With facts, examples, and arguments, he replaces Sadolet's idealized Catholicism with the abuses and corruptions of the papacy. Calvin even used the words of Reform-minded popes and bishops. He claimed the Word of God for the source of the Reformers' convictions. The Old Testament prophets who spoke out against corruption, often at the cost of their life, were the model for their own protest. He wrote with passion and power:

[5]Parker, 79.

As to your assertion that our only aim in shaking off this tyrannical yoke was to set ourselves free for unbridled licentiousness after casting away all thoughts of future life, let judgment be given after comparing our conduct with yours. We abound, indeed, in numerous faults; too often do we sin and fall. Still, though truth would, modesty will not permit me to boast how far we excel you in every respect, unless, perchance, you except Rome, that famous abode of sanctity, which having burst asunder the cords of pure discipline, and trodden all honor under foot, has so overflowed with all kinds of iniquity, that scarcely anything so abominable has ever been before.

Calvin's *Reply* arrived in Geneva on September 1, just months after a remarkable series of events that removed his previous opponents. His letter was widely circulated and received an enthusiastic reception. Sadolet would not even attempt a rebuttal to Calvin's arguments. Never again would Catholic authorities make a play for control of Geneva, which would remain a solidly Reformed city. Soon the tract found an audience beyond Geneva, serving to extend both the Reformation and Calvin's reputation as a controversialist.

Sixteenth-century Europe was a time of intense controversy with regard to religion. Political intrigue, harsh words, and even violent persecution were practiced by both sides. John Calvin flourished in this environment with his gift of writing letters, tracts, and sermons. The *Reply to Cardinal Sadolet* is a prime example. It remains one of the outstanding vindications of the Reformation. Like the Lausanne disputation, Calvin rose, almost unexpectedly, to the moment of need. His answer to God's call to stand for the faith produced an unforgettable event.

Calvin's season in Strasbourg was a time of recuperation and transformation. He flourished apart from Farel and under the watchful eye of Bucer. He developed his calling as a pastor, entered into family life, and matured as a writer. In many ways, he became a different man than the John Calvin who was thrown out of Geneva in 1538. One can see that time away from the town became God's hand in preparing him to return to the city.

12

Geneva: "Perfect School of Christ"

The congregation waited expectantly in the church of St. Pierre in Geneva. It was September of 1541, and John Calvin was back in the pulpit for the first time after his exile in Strasbourg. Many things had happened since he had left. What would he have to say in this first public address?

"Let us turn our attention to God's Word this day. I will begin my exposition by reading our text for the morning. . . ." John Calvin resumed preaching from where he had left off on Easter of 1538.

———

Calvin was back in Geneva to stay, and it would be his home for the next twenty-three years, until he died. He buried a wife and three children there. *The Institutes* matured and developed there. A huge volume of correspondence and his commentaries originated in Geneva. And he poured out his life developing a church that lived out the Reformed principles taken from the Bible. Never made a citizen of the city, Calvin still was its most influential resident.

For its part, Geneva, under his influence, became the center of the non-Lutheran Reformation in Europe and a haven for all manner of Protestant refugees fleeing persecution. It struggled to carve out its identity, newly independent in a tumultuous and often treacherous time. Forces inside the city and pressures from outside made the city like a storm-tossed boat on high seas.

Calvin and Geneva are names nearly synonymous during this period. Calvin was deeply involved in and influenced by the political currents of the town. Indeed, much has been made of his influence both positively and negatively. But Calvin cannot be reduced to one more small-town politician trying to impose his self-serving agenda on the populace. He was the leading pastor in a town going through significant changes. His care for his flock, his commitment to living out the Bible and challenging his people to do the same, and his strong following placed him center stage in all the events of the city. It was his convictions, not his ego or will-to-power, that made him forceful. To understand this, we must see John Calvin for what he was: a pastor and church Reformer.

When Calvin returned to Geneva from Strasbourg in 1541, organizing the Geneva church was the first order of business. On November 2, the Genevan *Ordannances* passed through the various councils and were enacted into law. In essence, they were identical to the reforms first proposed in 1537.

The church in Geneva was to live under the direction of four offices: pastors, doctors, elders, and deacons. Doctors were teachers, given the task of instructing believers in true doctrine and resisting error. Deacons provided care for the poor and the needy. The elders were laymen responsible for church discipline. There were to be twelve—all chosen from the various civil councils. Together with the pastors, they formed the *Consistoire*. This body, which always had more laymembers than clergy, was chaired by the elected Syndic, who was a member. The *Consistoire* met each Thursday and handled matters like non-attendance at church, contempt for church order, and unbecoming behavior. They had no power to summon offenders, though a council could do that on their behalf. Offenders who listened and agreed to obey the exhortations were dismissed. The stubborn had to be returned several times before being denied access to Communion and reported to the Little Council. It was clear that the *Consistoire* was a church court with no civil authority. Only the councils could press charges and pass sentences.

Finally, the pastors, of whom Calvin was but one, were responsible for preaching the Gospel, administering the sacraments, teaching believers the faith, training them in obedience, and caring for the sick and afflicted. A pastor was called by the company of pastors, a forerunner to the modern presbytery. It was the Little Council, though, that confirmed the call, authorized the ministry, and paid the salary. The *Ordan-*

nances also made it clear that the ministers were subject to Civil Law.

Matters of morals and church discipline were not foremost in the life of the pastors. Their primary work, according to the *Ordannances*, was to "proclaim the Word of God, to instruct, admonish, exhort and censure, both in public and private." The chief means for fulfilling this calling was by means of Bible exposition or preaching.

It was John Calvin's practice, as dramatically seen on his return to Geneva, to preach through entire books of the Bible section by section, and day by day. At first, he preached twice on Sunday and once on Monday, Wednesday, and Friday each week. On those weekdays, he expounded the Old Testament, and on Sundays, the New, though an occasional Sunday afternoon focused on a Psalm. By 1542 requests were made for even more preaching, a request that Calvin gladly obliged. In October 1549 the councils declared daily preaching. From that point on, Calvin preached twice on Sundays and every day of alternate weeks.

The year 1549 was significant with regard to Calvin's preaching for another reason. A group of Protestant refugees in Geneva hired a Frenchman by the name of Denis Raguenier to transcribe each sermon Calvin preached. Amazingly, he developed a system of shorthand that enabled him to write down sermons of some 6,000 words, often an hour in length, with a quill pen and ink in an unheated church winter and summer. So reliable was his system that Calvin himself did not revise or edit the copies. These transcriptions were bound and kept.

From this point, his preaching can be easily traced. From 1549 to 1554, Calvin preached 189 Sunday sermons on Acts, a shorter series on some of the Pauline letters between 1554 and 1558, and sixty-five sermons on the Harmony of the Gospels between 1559 and 1564. During this period, his weekday preaching included a series on Jeremiah and Lamentations, the Minor Prophets and Daniel (1550–52), 174 sermons on Ezekiel (1552–54), 159 on Job (1554–55), 200 on Deuteronomy (1555–56), 342 on Isaiah (1556–59), 123 on Genesis (1559–61), a short set on Judges (1561), 107 on 1 Samuel, 87 on 2 Samuel (1561–63), and a set on 1 Kings (1563–64). To quote T. H. L. Parker, "Those in Geneva who listened Sunday after Sunday, day after day, and did not shut their ears, but were 'instructed, admonished, exhorted, and censured,' received a training in Christianity such as had been given to few congregations in Europe."

Though by his own admission shy and reserved in person, Calvin could lose himself in the pulpit. His manner of delivery was lively, passionate, direct, and clear. They were not dry academic lectures, for this was the very Word of life. Calvin was coarse and angry at times, gentle and compassionate at others. He spoke clearly, and was attuned to the local idiom of his listeners. He was careful to illustrate technical words and convey shades of meaning, and sometimes he enacted conversations between opposing viewpoints with lively gestures.

Calvin preached without notes and directly from the Hebrew Old and Greek New Testament. That is not to say that he came unprepared or spoke extemporaneously.

> If I should enter the pulpit without deigning to glance at a book, and should frivolously think to myself, "Oh well, when I preach, God will give me enough to say," and come here without troubling to read or thinking what I ought to declare, and do not carefully consider how I must apply Holy Scripture to the edification of the people, then I should be an arrogant upstart.

Preaching in Geneva was not an isolated event, for congregational singing was included in Calvin's vision of church reform. For Calvin, there was a clear connection between the Gospel bringing joy to the hearts of people and that joy being expressed in song. He recognized the universal power in music to move hearts and for this reason considered it a great gift of God.

Simplicity in worship was important for Calvin. He preferred the singing of actual Psalms, "since the Holy Spirit himself has composed them. When we sing them, we are certain that God is putting words in our mouth and they are singing in us to exalt his glory." The music itself should not be "light and flighty" but should have weight and majesty as befits the worship of a mighty, redeeming God. The accompaniment was simple, harmony to be avoided.

Gone was the long Latin liturgy of the Roman Church. Instead, a typical Sunday morning service would have proceeded in this way:

The minister began with a set confession of sin in the name of the congregation, adding some verses of Scripture as he thought good, and then pronouncing the absolution (Declaration of Pardon) in the form: "To all those who in this way repent and seek Jesus Christ for their salvation, I pronounce absolution in the name of the Father, and the Son, and of the Holy Spirit, Amen." Hereupon the congregation sang the first four commandments and the minister prayed that these laws might be "written on hearts so that we may seek only to serve and obey thee." The rest of the commandments were sung as the minister entered the pulpit. He prefaced his sermon with the set prayer leading into the Lord's Prayer. Before the sermon began, however, the congregation sang a psalm and the minister prayed an extemporary prayer. After the sermon, an extemporary bidding prayer (which for Calvin began: "Now let us fall down before the majesty of our good God, praying him that he will give his grace not only to us but also to all people and nations of the earth. . . .") led into the long prayer beginning "Almighty God, heavenly Father, thou hast promised to hear our requests that we make to thee in the name of thy Son Jesus Christ, the well-beloved, our Lord," and praying for rulers, for pastors, and the Church, for the salvation of all men, for those in affliction, and especially for the persecuted under the Papacy, and for the salvation and sanctification of our own souls. The minister then gave a short explanation of the Lord's Prayer, and, after the singing of another psalm, dismissed the congregation with the Aaronic blessing. Apart from the singing and the sermon, the service was short, occupying less than a quarter of an hour.[1]

The reform of the Geneva church and its influence spread throughout Europe. The refugees, fleeing persecution in their homelands, eventually returned and carried with them the reforms they had seen firsthand. John Knox, the thundering Scot who brought the Reformation to Scotland, is an example. For three years, beginning in 1556, Knox served as pastor of the English-speaking congregation of refugees in Geneva. When opportunity came for him to return to Scotland, he established a national church fashioned after his Geneva experience. Geneva had been for him exactly what John Calvin had hoped for, "a more perfect school of Christ that ever was in the earth since the days of the Apostles."

———

Unfortunately, every school has its troublemakers, and Calvin was faced with continual opposition. Wherever and whenever the undisciplined willfulness and protected interests of one part of Geneva collided with the determination and intelligence of John Calvin, there was an explosion. Usually, this was in the areas of behavior and church discipline. The resistance was willing to allow Calvin to believe what he would, but when he expected conformity, even to God's Word, that was a step too far. Other resistance came from established families who saw the Reformation,

---

[1]Parker, 86–87.

and especially the growing number of refugees that followed Calvin, as a threat to their base of power in the city.

For example, in 1543 a question arose as to who had the authority of excommunication: the *Consistoire* or the Council?

> The Syndic who presided claimed it for the Council. Calvin objected, in his excitable manner, that they would have to kill or banish him first. Before the Syndics, he fully explained his position and "without any difficulty I have got what I asked for."[2]

By 1545 a diverse group of opponents began to coalesce into a more well-defined party that came to be called the Libertines. Comprised mostly of wealthy "old-guard" families, the Libertines chafed under Calvin's disciplined order that did not recognize rank or privilege.

Once this party strongly confronted Calvin, but it was not enough to overthrow him. A man by the name of Ameaux had been in trouble with the *Consistoire* on a periodic basis. One day in 1546, he spoke out against Calvin directly, calling him a bad man and a Frenchman with false doctrine. He was soon arrested by the civil authorities, tried by the Little Council, and sentenced to pay a heavy fine and make public acknowledgment of his errors. When the case was reviewed by the Council of 200, they reduced the sentence to a spoken apology to Calvin, who was standing before them at that time.

---

[2]Parker, 98.

Calvin refused the apology. Ameaux had called the Word of God "false doctrine," and, until the authorities set the situation right, Calvin would not enter the pulpit again. The city became agitated to the point of riot. The Council of 200 backed down and sentenced Ameaux to walk throughout the city in his shirt alone, carrying a torch and kneeling at prescribed places to beg God for forgiveness.

Issues and controversy continued to spring up over the years. Dancing, taverns, and public dramas all became points of contention between Calvin and the reforms he led and the Libertines with their desire for self-indulgence. It must be remembered that the Libertines did not oppose Calvin because they had a different plan for Geneva or the church. They simply resisted the restraints placed on them by the reforms. Calvin was the leader, so he became their target. Anyone, not just Calvin, who derailed the previously enjoyed privileges of class faced resistance.

13

The Strange Case of Michael Servetus

John Calvin was shocked to hear the news. Michael Servetus, the vocal heretic known and condemned throughout Europe, was seen in the congregation of St. Pierre while John preached on the afternoon of August 13, 1553. The report of his presence was from reliable people and was to be taken seriously.

Calvin immediately notified the authorities of Servetus' presence. In a rapid flurry of events, Servetus was discovered at the Inn of the Rose, where he had lodged overnight. As the magistrates made their arrest, Servetus was seeking the help of the innkeeper to hire a boat that could take him the next step in his clandestine journey to Italy. With his capture, John Calvin was unexpectedly thrown into the midst of another controversy. For the next two months, Servetus reviled Calvin, and Calvin's adversaries in Geneva used the opportunity to further undermine his efforts at reform.

Michael Servetus was a highly erratic personality. Considered brilliant in many regards, he constantly turned against the prevailing winds of his time with reckless abandon. The journey to Geneva and his plan to appear in the church where John Calvin was to preach was typical of the behavior that marked his strange and troubled life.

Servetus was born in the Aragon region of Spain around 1511, near the time that Ferdinand and Isabella were completing the unification of Spain as a nation, and some two decades after the royal couple had commissioned the voyages of Christopher Columbus. Though dominated by the Roman Catholic Church, this region had a heritage that included communities of Jews and Islamic Moors. This relative diversity of people, particularly of people who were non-Trinitarian monotheists, may have kindled the ideas that inflamed Servetus.

Servetus' early years were not unlike those of John Calvin. From an orthodox Catholic family, one of Michael's brothers was a lifelong priest who erected a special altar in their hometown. Michael spent his earliest years connected with a Franciscan monk who was confessor to the King of Spain. This king, Charles V, was the grandson of Ferdinand and Isabella as well as the chief benefactor of their achievements. The intellectual interests of King Charles and his court were deeply influenced by the Northern Renaissance humanist Erasmus. That sort of piety, undogmatic and spiritual, left room for rational enquiry while being secured to older ethical roots.

Servetus attended the University of Toulouse and studied law until 1529. While there, it seems that his wide-ranging mind first began to examine and then reject the doctrine of the Trinity. In 1531, his book *The Errors of the Trinity* was published in Basel, the most liberal city of the Swiss Reformation. In it, Servetus attacked the doctrine of the Trinity on every front. He denied that the Holy Spirit was a divine person of the Godhead. He spoke of the preexistent Word but denied that Jesus was the incarnation of the eternal Son. Indeed, one can scarcely distinguish between the Father and the Son except as different modes of divine activity. In addition, Servetus had a confrontational style that made any idea he presented land with an offensive explosion.

These views made Servetus immediately *persona non grata* in both Protestant and Catholic regions. He was forced to leave Basel immediately. Strasbourg would not receive him. Quintana, his sponsor in the Spanish court, was shocked by his book. Catholic theologian Leander, who had been Martin Luther's opponent at the Diet of Worms, read the book and declared he had never read anything more nauseating.

With such a reception to his ideas, Michael Servetus went into hiding. He eventually turned up in Paris under the name of Michael Villeneuve, professor of mathematics. While there, he took up the study of medicine with a good deal of success. His observations on the circulation of blood preceded William Harvey's work by nearly seventy-five years. He wrote a popular textbook on medicinal syrups. It was during this stay that he missed the aforementioned appointment with the newly converted John Calvin to discuss theology.

While much is unknown regarding this part of Servetus' life, we do find him connected to a new edition of Ptolemy's *Geography* in 1535. He seems to have wandered through several cities until 1545, when he settled in Vienne, a city in southeast France, and developed a large medical practice.

His theological musings continued unabated all the while. In 1546 he completed a volume titled *Restitution of Christianity*, in which he again attacked the doctrine of the Trinity and the Incarnation, as well as the practice of infant baptism, as three primary sources of the corruption of primitive Christianity. In addition, he strongly rejected predestination and accepted the merit of good works for salvation.

It was in 1545, while working on *Restitution*, that Michael Servetus began to correspond with John Calvin by writing him a letter containing three specific questions. Calvin responded with his answers. Servetus wrote back disputing Calvin's answers. Calvin answered with a more detailed response and, for good measure, with a copy of *The Institutes* in which Servetus could see Calvin's teaching in full. Servetus, not one to let someone else have the last word, filled the copy of *The Institutes* with comments and criticisms, prepared an essay of thirty chapters, and sent them all to Geneva. One can hardly imagine what Calvin must have thought when he received his *Institutes* back from Servetus with brazen and rude comments like "I have often told you that triad of impossible monstrosities that you admit in God is not proved by any Scriptures properly understood"; and "This shows that your knowledge is ridiculous, nay, a magical enchantment and a lying justification." Calvin dropped all correspondence with the heretic, but did write his friend Farel in 1546:

> Servetus lately wrote to me and coupled with his letter a long volume of his delirious fancies, with the Trasonic boast that I should see something astonishing and unheard of. He would like to come here if it is agreeable to me. But I do not wish to pledge my word for his safety. For, if he comes, I will never let him depart alive, if I have any authority.

Unable to find a willing publisher, Servetus continued in his medical practice. Ongoing revision of the manuscript saw the book grow to mammoth proportions. Before long it included a revised edition of the original *Errors of the Trinity*, seven more "books" on theological topics, thirty "letters," sixty signs of the antichrist, and a number of polemical essays aimed at particular Reformers. It was no surprise that reputable publishers shied away. Finally, seven years after his last correspondence with John Calvin, Servetus hired a printer, and one thousand copies of the book were produced and released anonymously.

The book was an immediate scandal. The comic situation was that no one in Vienne knew that the author was Dr. Villeneuve, physician to the archbishop, much less that Dr. Villeneuve was, in truth, the heretic Michael Servetus.

In Geneva, John Calvin, along with a number of the other Swiss Reformers, quickly made the connection regarding the author's identity. Servetus' previous correspondence and the reports of several refugees were enough to put the pieces together. John Calvin wrote to a cousin of his in Vienne, passing on incriminating information and scolding the Roman Catholic authorities for indulging the presence of such a heretic as Servetus. The cousin passed the information along, and soon the Viennese authorities investigated. Servetus was imprisoned and examined, but he maintained his identity as Villeneuve and denied all accusations with long and circuitous stories of his early years and travels.

While in captivity, Servetus made an early-morning escape, much to the chagrin of the local tribunal. Despite being without a prisoner, the Viennese condemned Servetus *in absentia* and on June 17, 1553, burned him in effigy with as many of his books as could be found.

Logic would dictate that Servetus should have understood, if not the error of his idea, at least the imminent danger of his situation. Instead, on August 13, less than three months later, he was found in Geneva preparing to listen to a sermon of John Calvin.

———

The trial of Michael Servetus began soon thereafter, when a servant of John Calvin brought thirty-eight criminal counts before the civil court. Most of them were of a theological nature, but it was almost universally accepted to be the responsibility of the civil government to prosecute heretics. Bringing the charges was a refugee employed by Calvin by the name of Nicolas de la Fontaine. As official accuser, it was required of him to join the accused in jail until he could furnish proofs.

As the case was prosecuted, there arose a sudden and surprising turn. Servetus replied to the charges with skill and actually began to establish a measure of credibility for himself in the face of the accusations. Had the trial of Michael Servetus been simply a matter of judging the charges of heresy, the entire procedure would have been short and swift. Servetus held views heretical to orthodox Christians of every party, and with no sign of repentance, there was never a doubt of his being a heretic. But something else began to eclipse the matter of heresy in the trial. It became an opportunity for Calvin's opponents: they became a sympathetic crowd for Servetus and used the trial as a means to further undermine Calvin's authority in Geneva.

On August 16 a new lawyer and close friend of Calvin, Germain Colladon, appeared to prosecute the case before Geneva's Little Council. Heated exchanges were the order of the day. The day's proceedings made it increasingly clear that Servetus might be the accused, but John Calvin was to be the defendant.

All this made for a very confusing situation. A majority of the Little Council was hostile to Calvin and his authority. But to resist him, they were forced to take sides with Servetus, a man of offensive temperament who was universally held by religious people to be an intolerable heretic and threat to society. Servetus' lawyer defended him "not because he believed in the accused but because he disliked the accuser."

By August 17 the magnitude of the matter was evident. John Calvin appeared in person to press the case before the Little Council. He pressed the attack on the matter of the Trinity. In addition, he pointed to the writings of Servetus that cast doubt on Israel as a land of "milk and honey," which undermined the reliability of Moses' writings under the inspiration of the Holy Spirit. Pushing further, Calvin challenged Servetus on his underlying pantheistic worldview. Servetus admitted that, in his belief, the floor and benches of the courtroom were "the substance of God."

"Then the devil is God in substance!" declared Calvin by deduction.

Servetus replied with a laugh, "Do you doubt it?"

Later that day, the Little Council relieved de la Fontaine from the responsibility of his charges, and put the State Attorney of the town in charge of the case. Four days after that, the Little Council decided to seek advice from four other Swiss cities as well as obtain court records from Vienne. This apparent bid for time was taken as an encouraging sign by Servetus and his supporters. Calvin wanted the court to convict the heretic immediately and felt that he had provided abundant proof for such a verdict.

On August 23 the city attorney attempted a new strategy and brought a new set of charges against Servetus. These were based on matters of personal character and the seditious influence of his teachings. While the heresy charges were not dropped, the theological details were minimized. The new tactic failed utterly. As a result, if Servetus was to be condemned, the theological charges would now have to stand alone. Finally, the points of contention were narrowly focused.

A week after this development, correspondence was received from Vienne. They had tried and condemned him, and now they wanted to make good on their decision and redeem the error of allowing his escape. They wanted Servetus extradited for execution. The Little Council politely refused and kept Servetus, while awaiting replies from the other cities.

Another decision was made to arrange for a public debate and presentation of Servetus' errors. The debate began on September 1, and Servetus immediately complained that the prison was not a suitable place for such a dispute. Calvin quickly agreed, seeing a chance to go before the public with an opponent he could easily discredit. Calvin's opponents, in turn, sensed this same opportunity for their disaster, so worked to cut short the debate. Calvin was finally ordered to present Servetus' errors in writing, to which Servetus was to reply in writing, and all in Latin!

Calvin quickly assembled the charges and the evidence from the writings of his opponent. Just as quickly, Servetus replied, declaring Calvin to be "a disciple of Simon Magus" (cf. Acts 8:4–25), "of confused mind . . . one who hopes by barking like a dog to overwhelm the judges." This statement was so offensive that all the pastors of Geneva and the surrounding area wrote and signed a sharp reply. Within three days, Servetus returned the letter covered with his notations and replies: "You lie"; "you play the fool"; "you rave"; "cheat"; and "vile scoundrel."

Somehow emboldened, Servetus sent an appeal to the Genevan government on September 22. In it he demanded that Calvin be arrested under the law of *lex talionis* as a false accuser and a heretic, and "that the case be settled by his or my death or other penalty. In this way," he said, "Calvin should be not merely condemned but exterminated and his goods given over to me!" On that day, the letters to the Swiss cities for their opinions were finally dispatched.

While all Geneva was aflame with interest in the trial of Servetus, another issue arose and intertwined itself with the challenge to Calvin's position and authority. It seems that since the beginning of the reforms in the city, a key point of disagreement had been between the civil authorities, who were now trying Michael Servetus, and the church authority, embodied in the *Consistoire*.

Under the previous Roman Catholic rule, civil and church government had been so welded together that the civil government had always enforced matters of religious excommunication. With the coming of Farel and Calvin and the *Ordannances*, the power of excommunication had been taken from civil government and placed in the hands of a new church body, the *Consistoire*. This transfer of power had remained a bone of contention just below the surface of life in Geneva.

The Reform Party and refugees were committed to the separation of powers, while the older families and entrenched powers resented their loss. With Calvin's authority besieged during the trial of Servetus, there was new opportunity to press the issue once again.

On September 1, the same day that Calvin and Servetus began their so-called debate, the aristocratic Philibert Berthelier appealed to the Little Council to overrule the *Consistoire*'s order of excommunication upon him and allow him to take Communion when it was celebrated in two days. In an ironic twist of issues, this same Berthelier spoke as Servetus' lawyer during the first days of the trial.

The Little Council met and reviewed the matter, and they asked Calvin for his input. This turn of events was as serious as it was sudden and unexpected. It represented a frontal attack on Calvin's reforms, his leadership, and his teaching. He spoke with great vehemence but ultimately lost. Berthelier was to be admitted to Communion on Sunday. The decision of the *Consistoire* was overruled even though Berthelier's life was notoriously corrupt.

Not to give up easily, Calvin managed an unusual Saturday meeting of the Little Council. "I would die before I would administer the sacrament to Berthelier!" he declared. For Calvin, too much was at stake with regard to the discipline of the church and the purity of the sacraments to be neutral. Still the Little Council was unswayed. Their previous decision was to stand and that was final. Or so it seemed.

In what we can only guess to be nervous expediency, members of the Council spoke privately with Berthelier and urged him in the strongest terms not to appear in church the next day. "Let it be enough that you have won," they counseled. "Don't press Calvin to a public confrontation!"

The next day, Calvin preached from the pulpit of St. Pierre's as was his custom. As he prepared to administer the sacrament of Communion to the congregation, he declared that he would never profane the sacrament by administering it to an excommunicated person. Then, raising his voice and lifting up his hands, he exclaimed in the words of the church Father Chrysostom: " 'I will lay down my life ere these hands shall reach forth the sacred things of God to those who have been branded as His despisers.' " Church historian Philip Schaff referred to this as "another moment of sublime Christian heroism."

Whether Berthelier chose not to appear in light of previous warnings, or whether, as some believe, Calvin's warning so moved his opponents that they restrained him, we can only guess. For whatever reason, Berthelier did not present himself, and there was no confrontation. The crisis was averted. Calvin prevailed by sheer weight of character. Beza records that Communion was celebrated "in profound silence, and under a solemn awe, as if the Deity himself had been visibly present among them."

A few days later, on September 7, Calvin and the ministers of Geneva lodged a formal protest with the Little Council regarding their decision. With no reply, the complaint was repeated a week later. Finally, on

September 18, the Little Council begrudgingly voted to "hold on to the *Ordannances* as before." The power of excommunication was once again in the hands of a church body and not held by the civil government. The principles of reform had weathered a major attack.

Throughout this entire side issue, there was still the major issue of Michael Servetus and his blistering exchange with John Calvin. No doubt some of his brazen replies had been emboldened by the matters related to Berthelier and his excommunication. However, all rudeness was drained from him on October 20, when the replies from the Swiss cities of Zurich, Basel, Bern, and Schaffhausen were read to the Little Council. They were unanimous and nearly uniform. The opinions of Michael Servetus were heretical and blasphemous.

Servetus apparently was truly surprised. At first crushed, he soon regained his composure, though never his belligerence. His supporters tried one last legal maneuver in an attempt to transfer his case to the Council of 200, but to no avail. On October 26 the Little Council declared a guilty verdict, and the next day sentence was passed. Servetus was to be burned to death the very next day. It was a sentence identical to the earlier one rendered in Vienne.

Servetus asked for and received one last meeting with John Calvin. Without retracting a single opinion, he did ask pardon for any wrong he might have done to Calvin, and also for an easier death. Calvin granted both, and made an appeal with the other ministers of Geneva that Servetus be beheaded instead. The plea landed on deaf ears and Servetus died as sentenced.

William Farel, who was in Geneva on the day and accompanied Servetus to the stake, heard his last prayer while the flames grew higher: "Jesus thou Son of the eternal God, have pity on me!" It was Farel's reflection that if Servetus was willing to confess Jesus, the eternal Son of God, he may have been saved.

The trial and death of Michael Servetus was not the central point of John Calvin's life and ministry, yet it has often been remembered and discussed. From our perspective and experience centuries later, such a gruesome turn of events seems harsh and unreasonable. Perhaps some reflections by noted Calvin scholars will help put both context and closure to this sad affair.

Biographer T. H. L. Parker writes:

> On the toleration of the punishment there will be a difference of opinion between the consensus of opinion in the twentieth century and the consensus of opinion in the sixteenth century. Our imaginations shudder at the terror and agony of the wretched victim. Their sense of order was horrified by the thought of souls destroyed by false doctrine, of Churches torn asunder into parties, of the vengeance of God displayed upon them in war, pestilence, famine.[1]

Alister E. McGrath says:

> The trial and execution of Michael Servetus as a

---

[1]Parker, 123.

heretic have, more than any other event, colored Calvin's posthumous reputation. It is not entirely clear why scholars have singled out the execution of Servetus as somehow more notable or significant than the mass executions carried out within Germany after the abortive Peasants' War (1525), and after the ending of the siege of Münster (1534), or the ruthless policy of execution of Roman Catholic priests in Elizabethan England. Even as late as 1612, the English secular arm, at the behest of the bishops of London and Lichfield, publicly burned two individuals who held views like those of Servetus. In France, similar ruthless policies of execution were employed: thirty-nine individuals were ordered to be burned at Paris for heresy between May 1547 and March 1550. . . .

The sixteenth century knew little, if anything, of the modern distaste for capital punishment, and regarded it as a legitimate and expedient method of eliminating undesirables and discouraging their imitation. The town of Geneva was no exception: lacking a long-term prison (short-term prisoners were held captive, at their own expense, while they awaited trial), it had only two major penalties at its disposal—banishment and execution. Nor is it entirely clear why the affair should be thought of as demonstrating anything especially monstrous concerning Calvin. His tacit support for the capital penalty for offences such as heresy, which he (and his contemporaries) regarded as serious, makes him little more than a child of his age rather than an outrageous exception to its standards.

Post-Enlightenment writers have every right to protest against the cruelty of earlier generations; to single out Calvin for particular criticism, however, suggests a selectivity approaching victimization. To target him in this way—when the manner of his involvement was, to say the least, oblique—and overlook the much greater claims to infamy of other individuals and institutions, raises difficult questions concerning the precommitments of his critics. Servetus was the *only* individual put to death for his religious opinions in Geneva during Calvin's lifetime, at a time when executions of this nature were commonplace elsewhere.[2]

14

Calvin's Death

It was late in the winter of 1564. John Calvin was in obvious pain and failing health. He had not preached at St. Pierre since February. He made few meetings and only rarely got out. His mind was clear and his thoughts focused, but his body seemed to run out of energy. He dictated his letters as best he could. And there were still pastoral duties to attend to. Even when encouraged to rest, he refused.

Calvin had never been a robust figure. As far back as his student days, he suffered with digestive problems and insomnia. Physical maladies had not seemed to hinder his work or ministry; they were simply overcome by his intense drive to duty. But barely past fifty years old, the problems seemed to accumulate and linger. A letter of February 1564 gave his own summary of his symptoms:

> At present, all these enemies charge me like troops. As soon as I recovered from a quartan fever [a recurring fever with two days between attacks; per-

haps a mild form of malaria], I was taken with severe and acute pains in my calves, which, after being partly relieved, returned a second and then a third time. At last they turned into a disease of the joints, which spread from my feet to my knees. An ulcer in the hemorrhoid veins long tortured me. . . . Last summer I had an attack of nephritis [an inflammation of the kidneys, perhaps Bright's Disease]. As I could not endure the jolting of the horseback, I was carried into the country in a litter. Coming home, I wanted to walk some of the way. I had hardly gone a mile when I was forced to stop, because of a feeling of lassitude in the loins, for I wanted to make water. And then, to my surprise, blood flowed instead of urine. As soon as I got home, I went to bed. The nephritis was very painful and remedies gave me only partial relief. At last, with the most painful strainings, I ejected a stone, and this lessened the evil. But it was so big that it tore the urinary canal and the flow of blood could be arrested only by an injection of woman's milk through a syringe. Since then I have ejected several others, and the heaviness of my loins is sufficient symptom that there is still some stone there.

On April 28 the ministers of Geneva gathered at the home of John Calvin. He was frail and weak, unable to get out of bed, but he was still clear of mind. They spoke and reflected together. Calvin had for several months mentioned his awareness of approaching death. This was the last time that he would meet with this group, the last time he would speak "publicly." Calvin relived his life in Geneva with these friends and colleagues. It was, in the words of T. H. L. Parker, "a strange medley of devotion, self-justification, and bitterness." It gives us insight into Calvin's own perspective on his life and work.

> When I first came to this church, I found almost nothing in it. There was preaching and that was all. They would look out for idols, it is true, and burn them. But there was no reformation; and everything was in disorder. . . .

> I have lived here amid continual strifes. I have been saluted in derision of an evening before my door with forty or fifty arquebus [a muzzle-loading rifle] shots. Just imagine how that frightened a poor scholar, timid as I am, and, as I confess, I have always been.

> Then afterwards I was expelled from this city and went to Strasbourg; and when I had lived there some time I was called back here. But I had no less trouble when I tried to do my duty than previously. They set the dogs at my heels, calling out, "Wretch! Wretch!" and they snapped at my gown and my legs. . . . So I have been amid struggles. And you will find that there will be others, not less, but greater. For you are a perverse and unhappy nation, and though there are good men in it, the nation is perverse and wicked, and you will have trouble when God shall have called me away; for though I am nothing, yet I well know that I have prevented three thousand tumults that might have broken out in Geneva. But take courage and fortify yourselves, for God will make use of this church and will maintain it, and assures you that he will protect it.

> I have had many infirmities which you have been

obliged to bear with, and what is more, all I have done has been worth nothing. The ungodly will greedily seize upon this word, but I say it again that all I have done has been worth nothing, and that I am a miserable creature. But certainly I can say this, that I have willed what is good, that my vices have always displeased me, and that the root of the fear of God has been in my heart; and you may say that the disposition was good; and I pray you, that the evil be forgiven me, and if there was any good, that you conform yourselves to it and make it an example.

As to my doctrine, I have taught faithfully, and God has given me grace to write what I have written as faithfully as it was in my power. I have not falsified a single passage of the Scriptures, not given it a wrong interpretation to the best of my knowledge; and though I might have introduced subtle senses, had I studied subtlety, I cast that temptation under my feet and always aimed at simplicity.

I have written nothing out of hatred to anyone, but I have always faithfully propounded what I esteemed to be for the glory of God. . . .

Let everyone consider the obligation which he has not only to this church but also to the city, which you have promised to serve in adversity as well as in prosperity. . . .

And study, too, that there be no bickerings or sharp words among you, for sometimes biting gibes will be bandied about. This will take place, it is true, in fun, but there will be bitterness in the heart. All that is good for nothing, and is even contrary to a Christian disposition. You should guard against it, and live in good accord and all friendship and sincerity.

I had forgotten this point: I pray you make no change, no innovation. People often ask for novelties. Not that I desire for my own sake, out of ambition, that what I have established should remain, and that people should retain it without wishing for something better, but because all changes are dangerous and sometimes harmful.

His old friend Farel later came to see him one last time. After the visit, Farel asked friends to pray for Calvin but not to visit. Calvin lingered in pain, trying to work while repeating verses from the Psalms.

Finally, on May 27, there was entered into the Register of the Geneva Council this note: "Today, about eight o'clock in the evening, John Calvin has gone to God whole and entire in sense and understanding, thanks be to God." By 2:00 P.M. the next day, wrapped in a simple shroud and placed in a simple wooden coffin, his body was laid to rest.

In modern-day Geneva there stands a monument to the Reformation that flowed through the city. Four men, Guillaume Farel, John Calvin, Theodore Beza, and John Knox are remembered in stone.

What a visitor will not find is the place where the body of John Calvin was laid to rest. He had left explicit instructions that he be buried in the common cemetery of Geneva with no tombstone. To this day, his gravesite is unknown.

Calvin wanted it that way. He neither feared death, nor cared to be remembered himself. No one would be more surprised than John Calvin that a legacy such as "Calvinism" would spring up behind him.

Years earlier, he had written in his commentary on Genesis 11:4, that

> The saying of Juvenal is known: "Death alone acknowledges how insignificant are the bodies of men." Yet even death does not correct our pride, nor constrain us seriously to confess our miserable condition: for often more pride is displayed in funerals than in nuptial pomp. By such an example, however, we are admonished how fitting it is that we should live and die humbly.

Appendix:
A Chronology of
Calvin's Writings

1532	*Commentary on Seneca's "De Clementia"*
1534	*Psychopannia*
1536	*The Institutes*—first edition
1539	*The Institutes*—second edition
	The Reply to Cardinal Sadolet
1540	*Romans*
1541	*The Institutes*—French edition
	A Small Treatise on the Lord's Supper
1546	*I Corinthians*
1547	*II Corinthians*
1548	*Galatians, Ephesians, Philippians &*
	Colossians, as one set
	I & II Timothy
1549	*Titus & Hebrews*
1550	*I & II Thessalonians*
	James
1551	*Catholic Epistles: I & II Peter, Jude*

158

1552 *Acts*—first volume
1553 *Gospel of John*
1554 *Acts*—second volume
      Genesis
1555 *Harmony of the Gospels*
1557 *Psalms*
      Hosea
1559 *The Institutes*—major revision
      Minor Prophets
      Isaiah—rewritten
1561 *Daniel*
1563 *Harmony of the Pentateuch*
      Jeremiah
      Lamentations

Posthumously:

1564 *Joshua*
1565 *Ezekiel 1–20*

Bibliography

Barton, Florence Whitfield. *Calvin and the Duchess.* Louisville, Ky.: Westminster/John Knox Press, 1989.

Bouwsma, William J. *John Calvin: A Sixteenth-Century Portrait.* Oxford: Oxford University Press, 1988.

Duffield, G. E., ed. *John Calvin: A Collection of Essays.* Grand Rapids, Mich.: Wm. B. Eerdmans Publishing Co., 1966.

Graham, W. Fred. *The Constructive Revolutionary: John Calvin and His Socio-Economic Impact.* Richmond, Va.: John Knox Press, 1971.

Keesecker, William E., ed. *A Calvin Reader: Reflections on Living.* Philadelphia, Pa.: Westminster Press, 1985.

McGrath, Alister E. *A Life of John Calvin: A Study in the Shaping of Western Culture.* Cambridge, Mass.: Blackwell Publishers, Inc., 1990.

McNeill, John T. *The History and Character of Calvinism.* New York: Oxford University Press, 1962.

Monter, E. William. *Calvin's Geneva.* New York: John

Wiley & Sons, Inc., 1967.

Mullett, Michael. *Calvin*. New York: Routledge, 1989.

Parker, T. H. L. *John Calvin: A Biography*. London: J. M. Dent & Sons, Ltd., 1975.

Reid, W. Stanford, ed. *John Calvin: His Influence in the Western World*. Grand Rapids, Mich.: Zondervan Publishing House, 1982.

Schaff, Philip. *History of the Christian Church*. Vol. VIII, chapters 8–14, Charles Scribners, 1910.

Schmidt, Albert-Marie. *Calvin and the Calvinistic Tradition*. New York: Harper and Brothers, 1960.

Steinmetz, David. *Calvin in Context*. Oxford: Oxford University Press, 1995.

Walker, Williston. *John Calvin: The Organizer of Reformed Protestantism*. New York: Schocken Books, 1906.

Christian History Magazine, vol. V, no. 4. This entire issue was dedicated to John Calvin, and includes a good number and wide variety of first-rate articles on Calvin's life, times, and writings. This issue is available on the *Christian History* CD-ROM of the magazine's first fifty issues.